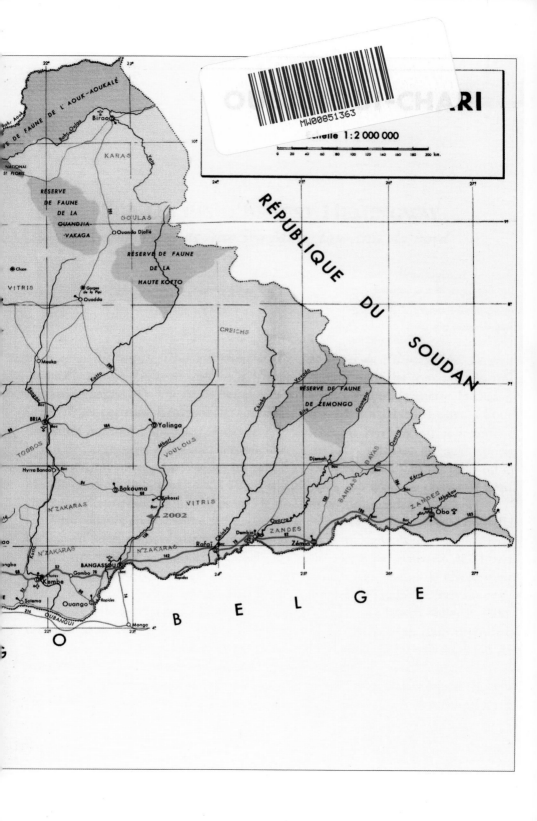

SPORTS AFIELD

THE PREMIER HUNTING ADVENTURE MAGAZINE

❏ Start or ❏ Renew my subscription at these special rates
❏ Enclosed is my payment of $24.97 for 1 year (6 issues)
❏ $47.97 for a 1 year international subscription PAYABLE IN U.S. FUNDS, NO BILL ME

❏ VISA ❏ MC ❏ DISCOVER #   Exp. Date MM/YY

NAME   (Please Print)

ADDRESS

CITY/STATE

POSTAL CODE/COUNTRY

6 ISSUES FOR $24.97

Sports Afield is America's Premier Big-Game Hunting Magazine!

SPORTS AFIELD, $6.99 single-copy cost. Your first copy will be on its way to you in 6 to 8 weeks. A publication of **FIELD SPORTS PUB, INC.**

SUBSCRIBE ONLINE!
www.sportsafield.com

TL0901

NO POSTAGE
NECESSARY
IF MAILED
IN THE
UNITED STATES

BUSINESS REPLY MAIL

FIRST-CLASS MAIL   PERMIT NO 24   SEAL BEACH CA

POSTAGE WILL BE PAID BY ADDRESSEE

**SPORTS
AFIELD**

PO BOX 2129
SEAL BEACH CA 90740-9972

SAFARI PRESS

Safari Press, America's premier sporting publisher, regularly releases books on worldwide big-game hunting, wingshooting, and sporting firearms. Return this postcard and you will receive our beautiful 40 page color catalog FREE.

PLEASE PRINT (block letters please):

First Name _____ Last _____
Address _____

City _____ State _____ Zip _____
Country _____
E-mail _____

Send a catalog to a friend:

First Name _____ Last _____
Address _____

City _____ State _____ Zip _____
Country _____
E-mail _____

www.safaripress.com   POSTCA

SAFARI PRESS

P.O. Box 3095

Long Beach, CA 90803-0095, USA

PLACE
POSTAGE
HERE

Breath of Africa

Breath of Africa

Beyond the Hunt—Chronicles of a Big-Game Hunter

by

Édouard-Pierre Decoster

Translated by

Chris Tina Anderes and Julia Monod Robinson

Safari Press

Breath of Africa © 2010 by Édouard-Pierre Decoster. Illustrations © by Gabriel Bernaldo de Quirós. No part of this publication may be used or reproduced in any form or by any means without permission from the publisher.

The trademark Safari Press ® is registered with the U.S. Patent and Trademark Office and in other countries.

Decoster, Édouard-Pierre

Second English edition

Safari Press

2010 Long Beach, California

ISBN 978-1-57157-342-1

Library of Congress Catalog Card Number: 2009918

10 9 8 7 6 5 4 3 2 1

Printed in China

Readers wishing to receive the Safari Press catalog, featuring many fine books on big-game hunting, wingshooting, and sporting firearms, should write to Safari Press Inc., P.O. Box 3095, Long Beach, CA 90803, USA. Tel: (714) 894-9080 or visit our Web site at www.safaripress.com.

Original French edition published as *Le Vent des Pistes* © 2003 by Édouard-Pierre Decoster. Translated from French by ChrisTina Anderes and Julia Monod Robinson.

Dedication

To Africa

And God made the beasts of the earth after his kind,
and cattle after their kind,
and everything that creeps upon the earth after his kind:
and God saw that it was good.

Genesis 1:27

Message from the Translators

When we were approached in the spring of 2007 to translate *Le Vent des Pistes*, we initially had a few reservations about a book on big-game hunting. We had scant sympathy for hunters of any stripe, and it was a subject about which we knew nothing. But then we read the book and were charmed by these stories and by the author's evident love of Africa. We set about learning more, devoured any literature we could find, bought specialized magazines, searched Web sites, watched nature programs on television with renewed interest, and reread the books to which the author likes to refer. As the translation progressed, it became clear that these stories are not just about big-game hunting; they are a tribute to a continent, its peoples, and glorious fauna. The book is also a call to arms, a plea for the preservation of the fragile balance of nature. We hope we have managed to convey intact the author's passion.

Table of Contents

Foreword

A seemingly insignificant detail occasionally provides a clue to a person's true nature. Who would have guessed that Hoggar, the magnificent gray stallion listed on a race program many years ago, had been named by his owner in memory of a stay in Africa in 1965, in the region of Tamanrasset. That first trip made such an impression on Édouard-Pierre Decoster that from then on he gave almost all his horses Berber names.

Eddy, as his friends know him, returned often after that first encounter with a continent that was to possess him throughout his life. On each expedition he delved deeper, hunting, learning, immersing himself in the colors and flavors of Africa. And indeed, although the stories told in *Breath of Africa* take place in and around the hunt, this is hardly a conventional book on big-game hunting.

What is important to the author is that hunting allows him to connect with this big continent; thus, the real subject of the book is Africa itself. The author has a deep love for Africa, clearly manifest in his lyrical descriptions of the landscape. His appreciation and fine knowledge of art provide a fount of visual associations: The changing sky of the Hoggar at sunrise is a Renaissance enamel; the grandiose Zambezi Valley and its luxuriant, myriad shades of greens, ochres, and browns, seen from up above, are an expressionist painting by Rothko. People are depicted with the same artistic sensitivity. He is put in mind of the moving grandeur of a Caravaggio when he recalls how, as he sat by the flickering embers of a fire one evening listening to Michel Kaouche's stories, the half-light carved his old friend's features, charging his eyes with shadow and mystery. At that very moment a lion roared in the distance, adding poignancy to the scene.

Of all the animals that fill the pages of *Breath of Africa,* the lion takes pride of place—perhaps simply because the author has always admired the noble animal, or perhaps because a certain encounter with a lion was one of the most moving episodes of his expeditions.

Africa transports Édouard-Pierre Decoster back to the days of early man—primitive, harsh, and brief. How many times did he whisper to himself the words of the French poet Victor Hugo, "And it was so in ancient times"? One such occasion was surely on that evening when he observed the locals by the fire as they prepared to feast on the choice parts of the Lord Derby eland he had just shot, a scene he imagined played out thousands of years before by Magdalenian[1] hunters. They too,

---

[1] Late Paleolithic cultures found in Europe and Asia between 14,000 and 9,500 BCE, best known for their cave paintings in southwestern France.

no doubt, would have looked up at the moon rising in the starry night and pondered the meaning of life.

A dawn, like any other African dawn that an ordinary onlooker might see as merely beautiful, stirs the author to describe it as a "piece of eternity." These three words convey the essence of *Breath of Africa*; they are the key to the spiritual message that is the leitmotif of these pages.

Is it not the African bush just before sunrise that recalls the first morning of creation? All of nature is at peace. The lion are silent, the antelope quiet, the temperature mild, the wind subdued, the insects vanished. It is the world before the Fall; for a moment it is paradise on earth.

For a moment only, though, for in the words of Zoumbala, his faithful Central African tracker, "In Africa the earth is often the color of blood." And we understand that the author is reminding us, with barely veiled emotion, that in Rwanda, where he had hunted peacefully in 1989, the Hutus three years later massacred a million Tutsis, to whom he pays a vibrant homage.

And it is Zoumbala who, on taking leave of his "boss," speaks these words whose simplicity belies their heartfelt intensity: "When you are back over there in Europe and you feel your heart beating faster, you will know Zoumbala is thinking of you."

The book closes on today's Africa. The author does not embellish reality. He deplores the tribal wars, the misconceived development that is ruining vast regions. He condemns the destruction of the big-game animals, not only by poachers but also by hunters driven by monetary gain or obsessive trophy hunting, the kind who shoot from their vehicles. But he also knows that some African countries have understood the importance of managing the treasure that their magnificent wildlife represents, and that big-game hunting has its role to play, so long as it is practiced ethically. With care, Africa will remain a land of adventure in the best sense of the term. For, despite today's easy traveling, it will always be a place apart.

Some books are too rich for a single reading. *Breath of Africa* is such a book.

Philippe Rambaud
Hunting and Art columnist
Alumnus, Ecole du Louvre, Paris
March 2008

Preface

I would dearly have loved it had Ernest Hemingway done me the honor of writing a few words of introduction to these tales. I have the greatest admiration for this man who wrote so much, so beautifully, and with such apparent ease. Unfortunately, he was away on safari[2] in a far-off land, and I received a reply saying that he would be incommunicado for some time.

I haven't had much luck with Mr. Hemingway. Indeed, I just missed him at Mto Wa Mbu[3] Camp, then at Las Ventas[4], and again at Bodeguita del Medio[5], where the acrid smell of his cigar still hung in the air. But I haven't given up hope; one day no doubt. . . .

As for Joseph Conrad, to whom I would also have happily appealed for a good word, he was off, I was told, sailing the infinite seas, far from conventional modes of communication.

And therefore, Dear Reader, I am obliged to put off to some later edition a preface worthy of your expectations. Meanwhile, I invite you to embark on this journey to Africa, but before you start turning the pages of these stories, I will dash off a few words of my own:

Since that day, millions of years ago in the Rift Valley, when man first stood erect, hunting has been the instrument of his evolution. Sharing the life of the hunters of Africa takes you back to that place in time when survival was the first and foremost preoccupation of *Homo habilis* and those who came after him.

The cave paintings that have come down to us from thirty thousand years ago and more, the earliest messages left by our distant ancestors, show that the hunt was central to their lives. These hunters were the first storytellers.

Our own little individual sparks of life have been passed down to us through an amazing succession of chance events in which the capture of a prey may have played a determining role. By being swifter than the gazelle,

---

[2] Safari means journey in Swahili.
[3] A village in northern Tanzania.
[4] A bullfighting ring in Madrid.
[5] One of the most famous Cuban restaurants in the world as well as an obligatory stop-off for all artists and writers who visit Havana.

more cunning than the lion, and stronger than the buffalo, our ancestors were able to safeguard the fragile thread that will ensure the continuity of our species on through time.

These tales are dedicated to the memory of all those who, over the years, be it for but a brief moment, have shared my journey along the perilous but fascinating path of life.

Lausanne, Switzerland
June 2003

Acknowledgments

I am indebted to Pierre Favre for assisting me
in the production of this book.

Tamanrasset
Tambacounda
Ouagadougou
Pendjari-Park
Cotonou
Garoua
Bamingui
Bakouma
Douala
Bangui
Nairobi
Equator
Yokadouma
Kigali
Arusha
Dar es-Salaam
Lake Cabora Bassa
Victoria Falls
Chimoio
Pretoria

The Gates to Atlantis

Into Africa:
Southern Algeria, Tamanrasset Province, 1965–1966

I was in a hurry to be outside, to get back to my stars, because that's what our old Africa is all about, isn't it, if you know how to look at her properly.

Romain Gary
The Roots of Heaven

It was like being on the moon. Lit by myriad stars, the silhouette of Mount Ilamane rose up like the crenelated donjon of a fortress. Standing at the edge of the foothills of the Atakor Range, it dominated the granite plateau of the Tefedest. A mass of scree draped its base like a stone *gandura*[1] lying crumpled at its feet.

The night was cold. The moon rose and the light became stronger; shapes seemed to come to life as we drew closer. The basalt contracted as it cooled, squeaking under our feet like frost. Delivered from the sun's tyranny, the desert teemed with life, resonating with hundreds of sounds that rang out in the darkness like fragments of crystal striking an ocean of hard rock. The night sounds, as they came forth, surreptitiously awakened deeply ingrained memories of what had once been one of the most fertile lands on the whole African continent.

From a distance came the high-pitched bark of a startled fennec (small African fox) and the sound of pebbles sliding, set in motion by a furtive passing shadow.

---

[1] See Glossary for this and other terms.

The Atakor Range.

We were on another planet, surrounded on all sides by stars that seemed so close I might have reached out and plucked one. No sky is more star studded, no sky brighter, than the skies over the Tropic of Cancer. I was filled with contentment at the sight of this magical spectacle. But, low on the horizon, the Southern Cross was already slipping away, a sign that dawn was near. A light north wind brought us the smell of cold ash rising from the volcanic rock, baked over and over by the infernal heat that had been vitrifying the Sahara since time immemorial.

Day broke and the sky metamorphosed. Like a jeweled Renaissance enamel, shades of wine red, cobalt blue, and milky white floated on a translucent background tinged with pink gold, dotted with a few stars that refused to be extinguished.

The *imrad* led the way, perched elegantly astride his *tarik*, the red and green leather decorated with geometric black patterns. The front of the saddle bore a trilobate, cross-shaped pommel covered in chiseled brass, a reminder to these fierce nomads of their Carthagenic ancestors' cult of Tanit, the goddess of the moon, the stars, and the night. Swaying along on his *mehari*, he seemed to be sailing over the dunes that bordered Erg Arechchoum. An *akli* dressed in white followed on foot, flanked by the three dogs that his master had entrusted to his care.

In the twilight the group looked like a sculpture and reminded me of the Léon Bureau[2] bronze in the summer drawing room of our family château in Bas Berry in central France, the home I'd left almost a year before. It belonged to the past and I quickly suppressed the memory of that distant paradise. I drove my mount a little harder than necessary, more to leave behind my melancholy thoughts than to catch up to the others, whom my camel was following docilely.

We were traveling through the upper reaches of Wadi I-n-Amguel, where a few young Haratin had brought their sheep and goats to drink at the rare *gueltas* that still held a little brackish water. There had been no real rain for over three years on this northern face of the Hoggar.

Aloof, the *imrad* did not speak a word. He paid us no particular attention, behaving as if he were alone in a world of which he was sole master. He rode with his eyes fixed on the horizon, turning only briefly in our direction to check

---

[2]Léon Bureau: nineteenth-century French sculptor of animals.

on the dogs that trotted along stiffly in the coolness of the morning. On his left wrist he wore a red jasper bracelet, and in the same hand he held the rein. The camel's light tan coat blended perfectly with the medley of ochres revealed by the breaking day. In his right hand he carried a spear bound in the center with leather, its silvery metal tip glinting like a rock crystal brooch.

With his white burnous and indigo-dyed tunic, the Targui cut a fine figure. The *akli* progressed with somewhat less panache, walking with a jerky gait and carrying his master's *takouba* (a superb sword with a haft of yellow amber, its blade grooved down the middle and engraved with the stylized outline of a lion). His Negroid features testified to Sudanese origins. He was probably the son of a black slave kidnapped by the Blue Men (Tuareg) during a *razzia* on the Mali or Niger border. Such raids were still relatively frequent in the early 1960s, and no one openly objected to the practice, ever since Father Charles de Foucauld[3] had been assassinated near his hermitage at Assekrem some fifty years earlier for having tried to resist.

The scenery through which we traveled was grandiose: Isolated sugar-loaf peaks were planted in a bed of saffron-streaked lava that veered to chocolate in the shade. Some of the strange mountain faces were eroded to such an extent that they resembled giant organ pipes abandoned to the rigors of elements heedless of their splendor.

As the camel track climbed higher it petered out, and it was only thanks to long experience that our guide managed to find his way through the maze of dunes and rubble that hindered our progress. In some places we worked our way through cliffs so steep-sided that the sun's rays reached us only when it was directly overhead.

On the *reg*, the only sign of life consisted of scant tufts of grass growing here and there among acacias mutilated by the shepherds who hacked off branches to feed their accursed goats, the scourge of the Sahelian regions. As we rode by,

[3]Charles de Foucauld (1858–1916) started out as a cavalry officer before renouncing the dissolute army life to take up orders. He settled in Tamanrasset, where he lived as a hermit, devoting his life to meditation. He was assassinated by pillagers in 1916. His influence made a lasting mark on Christian spirituality in the twentieth century. In 1966 I was among a handful of soldiers representing France at a commemoration of the fiftieth anniversary of his death.

The imrad.

white-collared black crows lumbered off into the air, reproaching us with their sinister cawing.

Animal carcasses littered the ground. Many of these were the remains of little donkeys that had been abandoned by their owners. Sun-bleached bones pierced their dried skin, as if the poor beasts had succumbed to an implosion. Across the track a little farther on lay the skeleton of what must once have been a dromedary. Its broad, sardonic grin seemed to be sending us a warning.

I was beginning to feel apprehensive.

Only the little black caravan bird, a charming white-headed desert passerine that fluttered around our caravan and escorted us from time to time, seemed to welcome our presence. As we entered a narrow defile, some Tifinagh characters engraved in the soft sandstone appeared to catch the *imrad*'s attention, but he did not seem to attach any particular importance to them, and so I paid them no notice.

We continued on through an ocean of sand spiked with bizarrely shaped pinnacles that the wind had chiseled through the ages into arches and ogives and sculpted with foliage and arabesques. It looked as though some titanic surrealist sculptor had been at work. A dry heat had now replaced the biting cold of the dawn, and it was rapidly getting hotter.

"*Alenkad!*" The *imrad* had spoken.

"*Alenkad!*" again.

At his words, the dogs emerged from their lethargy.

Less than a hundred yards away, a group of about ten dorcas gazelle were nibbling peacefully at the leaves of the white acacias. Some stood tall on their hind legs, stretching to get at the top shoots that were beyond the reach of the goats of the Haratin. These graceful little creatures were tiny, almost miniatures, hardly bigger than our dogs. With their tawny coats that shaded into sandy beige on the flank and then to white on the belly, and their charming curved-back, lyre-shaped horns, they reminded me of the figurines you see in nativity scenes at Christmas in our part of the world.

At a sign from his master, the *akli* released the hounds. They leaped into action like thoroughbreds at a gallop, propelling themselves with their powerful hind legs, which they swung forward almost to their muzzles before coming down on their forelegs, the pendulum movement generating greater momentum with every stride.

The sloughis were rapidly catching up to the dorcas. The Targui (singular for Tuareg) followed at a distance so as not to alert the small gazelle, which were still unaware of impending danger. Senses keen, he prepared to thrust his spear into the shining flank of one of the delicate animals.

The fastest dog was now no more than thirty yards or so from the throat of his prey, closing in fast like an eagle diving for the kill. Nothing would now halt the sacrifice that unfolded before me as I watched, deeply moved. And then, out of nowhere, came the sound of galloping horses. Two white-turbaned Blue Men on horseback appeared as if by magic. With their long, multi-tailed whips, they firmly stopped the pack and made it back off, allowing the small gazelle to escape their dire fate. Away they bounded like automated figures on springs.

One of the newcomers exchanged a few words with the *imrad,* who immediately had the slave leash the hounds. Showing not the slightest sign of vexation, he turned the camel round and, with the fatalism that is so typical of Africans, set off the way we had come.

It was clear that we were on forbidden territory!

Shortly afterward, as we again passed by the red sandstone rock that marked the entrance to the gorge, the slave pointed out to me the Tifinagh characters that we had ignored on the way in. In rudimentary French he explained that we had crossed into the *amenokal*'s territory, where no vassal was authorized to hunt.

I could not help feeling that the shadow of Antinea, the enigmatic queen of the hidden kingdom of Atlantis, lingered over these sun-drenched plateaus that day. We were at the southernmost edge of the Sahara, and the simoom, which was blowing up from Niger, brought us the hot breath of Black Africa.

I-n-Amguel, Algeria, November 1966

The Lion and the Warthog at the Faleme River

Eastern Senegal

To Yves, François, Gilbert, and all the others who were with me on this first lion safari.

We were young in those days, cocky and brimming with self-assurance. Our safaris were improvised affairs. Of all our carefree escapades, one of the most memorable was the time we took part in a lion hunt.

Antelope and gazelle were relatively rare in eastern Senegal and so the lion, finding themselves short of food, had got into the habit of raiding the cattle of the villagers, who had come to us for help in fighting off the terrifying predators. In exchange, borrowing a page from *The Magnificent Seven,* the people offered us bed and board and put us up in the village school, which was empty as school was out.

During the long, eventful trek, luck made up for our lack of experience. Led by their roaring, we happened upon a couple of lion drinking at the Faleme River. My buddy, Yves, took a hurried shot but was let down by a badly tuned gun and probably—understandably so—also a little flustered by the excitement of the moment. He missed the animal, which disappeared into the high grass growing along the river.

We had come within a hair's breadth of an amazing feat . . . of glory, even! Disappointed, we went back to our comrades-in-arms, who had a hard time believing us when we recounted our adventure.

The following day, admittedly a little late, we zeroed the rifle properly and got an unfortunate warthog right between the eyes, at the exact same spot where the previous day's lion had narrowly escaped his death.

The exceptional tusks on this warthog each measured fourteen inches.

I would have liked to bring back the animal's tusks, but to my great disappointment, the Africans accompanying us (dyed-in-the-wool Muslims) categorically refused any contact with the "unclean" creature. In their own jargon, they had me understand that the warthog should be left where it lay as an "offering to the lion." No doubt they hoped that the big cat would show its gratitude by sparing their cattle, at least for a time.

The years have gone by; one safari has followed another. I often think of the lion at the Faleme River, and although I've encountered many others since then, the image of that regal animal drinking at daybreak alongside his proud mate is engraved in my memory forever. And if the lion king, in order to satisfy his hunger for meat, occasionally dispatches a poor cow belonging to our friends the villagers, so be it.

Tambacounda, Senegal, May 1988

Postscript:

Ever since this little misadventure, I am careful to zero my rifle before chasing after lion. And this habit was to save my life on the banks of another river, as we will see in a later chapter.

Akagera Game Reserve

Rwanda

*These events put me in mind of Kurtz's last words to Marlow
in Joseph Conrad's* Heart of Darkness:
"The horror! The horror!"

The tiny African state of Rwanda just happens to be situated at the heart of the Great Lakes region, one of the most enchanting regions of sub-Saharan Africa. It sits to the west of legendary Lake Victoria, and its language is French, a result of its becoming a Belgian protectorate after the Great War.

This beautiful little country was once very densely populated. Hutus—the majority—and Tutsis coexisted as best they could. The Tutsis, also known as Watusis, came from the ancient kingdom of Nubia in the tenth century, and legend has it they are descendents of Ham, Noah's second son. The curse of Ham (also called the curse of Canaan) refers to the curse that Noah, Ham's father, placed upon Canaan, Ham's son, after Ham came upon his father drunk, naked, and sleeping. The curse of Ham was used to justify slavery and racism; the story is found in the book of Genesis 9:20–27.

Their noble features and exceptional height set the proud, nomadic Tutsis apart from other indigenous tribes. Early explorers were fascinated by these giants among men, and called them the "Masters of Africa."

The area is known as the Land of a Thousand Hills and is dotted with crystal-clear lakes from which spring a multitude of rivers that are among the innumerable sources of the White Nile. It used to be home to all kinds of animals, and you would encounter large Cape buffalo, topi, zebra, impala, and

I have often wondered about the fate of these young Tutsis on the banks of Lake Lulama. Were they among the million victims in the bloodbath of the Rwandan genocide a few years later? This photograph is a tribute to them in the name of all those who died. They will live on forever in our memories.

many, many others. Akagera Game Reserve, where hunting was allowed, takes its name from the river that flows through it en route to Lake Victoria.

At the end of the 1980s Rwanda was a peaceful paradise and one of Africa's most stable and best-structured countries. Many called it the Switzerland of Africa. It was in these green hills that I killed my first buffalo, an old coal-black bull that, I must admit, made a rather unexceptional trophy.

The former Rwandan president, Juvenal Habyarimana, an enlightened Hutu, understood early on that it was in the best interest of his small state to protect and manage its extraordinary wild animal populations. In the north, on the border with Uganda and Congo, he built Volcanoes National Park as a vast gorilla reserve, where the good-natured but endangered primates could live in peace, safe from poachers.

To symbolize his love of wildlife, he had the "world's largest" buffalo stuffed and mounted. It was in fact an old, rather ordinary buffalo cow, but had immensely long, though rather spindly, horns. She stood, proud and lifelike, in her glass case in the center of the arrivals hall of Kigali's brand-new airport, as if welcoming the visitors arriving from all over the world.

Kigali, Rwanda, 1989

Postscript:

For us travelers, nothing at the time suggested that this little haven would shortly afterward become a living hell. The appalling genocide of a million Tutsis by the blood-thirsty Hutus (called Operation Zero Tutsis) was to have dire consequences for the animals in Akagera Game Reserve, which found itself at the heart of the conflict. The wildlife sanctuary was brought to the brink of total destruction by an atrocious tribal war.

The Accident

Central African Republic

In Africa, the earth is often the color of blood.

Zoumbala

In 1991, on the very day President Bush (Senior) launched his invincible armada against Saddam Hussein's army of invasion, we landed in the north of the Central African Republic[1]. We had come to the banks of the Youhamba River looking for lion and giant eland, two of western Africa's most prized trophies.

On arrival we made the acquaintance of a professional big-game hunter, Michel Kaouche, an unconventional figure who was to give me a startling new perspective on big-game hunting. Under his guidance I would learn the real

---

[1]Several years after gaining independence, the former French colony of Ubangi-Shari, which had become the Central African Republic, was to be the theater of a coup d'état fomented by a former French army sergeant, Jean-Bedel Bokassa of the Mbaka tribe, an odd, Ubuesque character. In 1977 Bokassa proclaimed himself emperor and, with the help of France, organized a costly, burlesque coronation ceremony. In the full dress of an Empire Marshal (a replica of that worn by Marshal Ney for the coronation of Napoleon I), he was crowned before ten thousand guests of all nationalities.

Toward the end of the 1970s, this bloodthirsty clown took a personal part in the massacre of some one hundred students who were demonstrating against his tyrannical regime. In Bangui, when I visited there, it was even rumored that some of the bodies of these hapless youths had ended up in the imperial freezers. This would hardly have been surprising, as the Mbaka tribe is known for its cannibalistic practices. It was also hinted that certain French dignitaries posted in C.A.R. had unwittingly partaken of this human flesh. Weary of the barbarity, France arranged to have the buffoon deposed and forced him into exile in Ivory Coast.

thing. Here, on the Youhamba and in its *bakos*, was the heart of Africa, Joseph Conrad's heart of darkness.

On the third or fourth day, Yando, the first tracker, woke us very early. He said he had heard a lion's roar, "a big voice," far in the distance, as far as sound could carry. Michel immediately woke up the rest of the team. Besides Yando, we had two more trackers, Zoumbala and Pascal, and a driver named Alphonse, an old-timer with whom I hit it off immediately.

We were on the move, picking our way carefully through the dark, when we heard a roar, still far away. I am at a loss to describe how unnerving is that deep, echoing rumble when it rises from the depth of the African bush at night. Romain Gary in *The Roots of Heaven* called it "The only voice that can be raised towards the starry heavens without seeming ridiculous."

From time to time Zoumbala would call the animal on his *olifant*, a calling device covered with antelope skin. The lion answered with angry roars.

Daylight finally came, and at last we could make out our surroundings. The bush was alive with a hundred different sounds. Guinea fowl took flight and little antelope fled, telling us that the big cat was getting near.

My heart was racing. Hidden behind a termite mound, I crouched next to Alphonse, slightly behind the rest of the group. Michel was with Oliver, the hunter who had the heavy responsibility of shooting the animal, which was visible now as it glided through the thin vegetation faintly lit by the first light of dawn.

Oliver took his shot, but the cat, showing no reaction, set off at a steady trot in the direction of the high grass nearby. However, our trackers very quickly pointed out barely visible droplets of blood marking the path the animal had taken. Michel grumbled at the bad shot, and, even today, years later, I can still hear him muttering, "Now we've got ourselves a whole new problem."

The lion was wounded. For long hours we had been following his tracks through the thick forest that bordered the river. We were exhausted, parched. Michel and his trackers, concentrated and silent, were picking out the tracks left by the fugitive as he slipped away before us. Over and over they lost the slender thread that connected us to him, then found it again.

Night was about to fall again on the bush. Zoumbala and I were well ahead of the rest of the group, quickening our pace to try to cut off the lion's escape before darkness forced us to give up.

"I realized that the unthinkable was about to happen."

I heard the animal first as he progressed through the dry leaves covering the ground. Then I glimpsed him in the shadows of the *bako*, coming toward me at an easy, purposeful trot. Close to the ground, head raised, slit eyes vacant, he seemed to glide toward us. Toward me. I was no longer the hunter but the hunted, prey to Africa's most powerful cat.

My first bullet pierced his belly, bringing a terrifying growl of pain. Panicking, I missed my second shot, and he was already pouncing, his eyes alight. I saw no hate in them, only awareness and resolve: He was not going to give in without a fight.

At that precise instant I realized that the unthinkable was about to happen. I felt his fangs tearing into my flesh. My hand and the useless rifle it held were mashed in the cat's jaws. I smelled his fetid breath. I knew I was done for. But then, by some miracle, he spun around and fell dead on his side, taking me down with him. Blood flowed from his breast and mingled with my own that poured from the bites covering my arms.

Later I was told that the only thing I said to Zoumbala, who ran to me shouting, was, "Zoumbala, am I dead?"

The Banda tribesman kicked at the ground to uncover some rust-colored earth, and gave me this sibylline answer: "In Africa, boss, the earth is often the color of blood."

It was completely dark now along the Youhamba River, the darkness all the heavier here in the *bako*'s tropical vegetation. The lion lay dead on a bed of dry leaves. I could hardly see it in the dark. I bore it no grudge—after all, it had only been trying to save its skin!

My companions arrived quickly on the scene. I leaned back against the trunk of a tree that had been uprooted by elephant and sipped the cognac they poured me.

I can't say I have ever really enjoyed cognac, but that evening I did find the strong liquor tremendously comforting. It coursed gently through my bruised body like warm lava, reviving me. All these years later, I remember the brotherly compassion I felt at that moment for the soldiers of the Great War, for whom a few sips of brandy were perhaps the last thing they enjoyed before going to their horrible deaths in the muddy trenches of Argonne.

Supported by Yando and Zoumbala, I crossed the river one last time and we made our way back to camp, several kilometers away. I knew that I'd had a very narrow escape and resolved that from that day on I would live every day of my life as a great gift of Providence.

Thanks to an alert radio operator who by chance intercepted a message, we heard the throb of a small plane's engines in the early morning as the bush awakened. Then I found myself in the hospital in Bangui—surely the worst danger of all!—and then aboard a jet headed for France with two disagreeable nurses attending me. I managed to overhear them lamenting the fact that it was the lion that had died rather than me, the despicable hunter. And perhaps rightly so. Who knows? Maybe one day I, too, would regret not having met such an end, so terrifying and yet so like the fate of early man, whose life was a never-ending battle against all sorts of ferocious, bloodthirsty predators. These days, such a thrilling death is not so commonplace.

After a few weeks in the hospital, I was ready to set off again for Africa, which I was growing to love more and more with each passing day.

Bangui, Central African Republic, 1991

A Lion
in Sologne

France

Fear purifies the soul.

Masai Proverb

had a group of friends with whom I occasionally went after wild boar in Sologne, a well-known hunting region about sixty miles to the south of Paris, in France's Loire Valley. Toward November of the same year in which I had the close call with the lion, they insisted I accompany them.

It was the time of year when the forests of Sologne are at their best. Adorned with the first colors of fall, the leaves of the great sessile oaks rustled in the light breeze, creating a bucolic decor conducive to daydreaming. This was the stamping ground of Meaulnes[1], Alain Fournier's romantic protagonist, with whom I seemed to have so much in common.

Paradoxically, it was the wind that broke the spell, bringing me a sound I knew well but one so unexpected in this place that at first I refused to believe my ears. Though far distant and very faint, I thought I heard a lion roar!

A few dozen yards to my right stood a very old friend of mine who had often traveled with me in Africa. Disregarding safety procedures that I was normally the first to insist upon, I left my post and hobbled over to him with my cane.

"Did you just hear a lion roar?" I asked him.

No reply.

---

[1]*Le Grand Meaulnes,* a very successful novel by French author Alain Fournier (1886–1914), describes a romantic young man's journey of discovery in his quest for love.

"I thought I heard a lion roar!"

For his part, he was abiding by the rules, so he merely gave me a look of deep concern and mild disapproval—the kind of look you would give someone who was not quite right in the head. I let it drop and hurried back to my post.

From time to time shots rang out as animals passed by, most of them negotiating the line of fire unscathed. Then I heard a second roar, and shivered.

On my left was a charming young lady in whom I knew I had a sympathetic ear. I moved closer. "Excuse me, Alice, did you by any chance hear a lion roar just now?"

Somewhat surprised, she stared at me and then, with a ravishing smile, replied, "Don't worry, Eddy, there's only us here. Go on back to your post."

Despite the nice way she put it, it was clear that she too thought I was hallucinating, still traumatized by my hand-to-hand combat with the Youhamba lion. Slightly sheepish but unconvinced, I limped back to my post.

It was the last battue of the day, and afterward we all made our way to a small red-brick lodge with tufa-stone lintels, typical of the region, where our host's wife had prepared the customary refreshments. There, as always, amid the din of excited voices, everyone was recounting how he or she had "brought down" or "just missed" a deer, a boar, etc.—always with a good excuse, of course.

As for me, I was keeping a little apart from the others but not too far from the lovely Alice, and avoiding any talk of lion roaring, when I saw the pompous figure of the hunt leader, glass in hand. The man, a farmer with a stentorian voice, was discoursing authoritatively on the events of the day.

I had to get to the bottom of the matter and decided I needed his opinion to set my mind to rest. I approached him discreetly. Making sure no one else overheard, I ventured, rather timidly, "I hope you don't mind my asking whether you heard any lion roaring during the last battue?"

Irritated at the interruption, he gave me a withering look and declared in that certainty of tone of he whom nothing can surprise, "Well, of course you can hear 'em when the wind is blowing this way. They belong to the lion tamer. Everyone around here knows that, for heaven's sake!"

I was reassured—for the time being at least—that my senses were quite sound, though I was somewhat worried about my friends, who had been hunting regularly in the area for many years!

Sologne, France, November 1991

Eland at the Ends of the Earth

Kaga Nze Camp
Central African Republic

*God created the elephant, the lion, and the giant eland
to remind man of his limits.*

African Proverb

Kneeling on the sandy bed of the *mayo* where a few patches of dampness lingered, Yando dug vigorously with his ever-present machete. Exhausted by an interminable trek, Michel and I had sought shelter in the sparse vegetation that survived along the banks of the Koukourou. The brush protected us from the sun and the insects, and at the same time hid us from the keen eyes of the Lord Derby eland we'd been tracking since first light.

I watched the tracker as he dug at the ground. He was searching for water the way animals do. He had a variety of often surprising uses for the rudimentary tool that accompanied him everywhere: He trimmed his nails with it, and used it as an ax, a spade, a tire iron, and, when the need arose, as a fearsome weapon. My eyes followed the movement of the machete; it was part of him, a remarkably efficient extension of his arm.

The herd stood just a few hundred yards from our makeshift encampment, but we were upwind. We sat and waited. The old hunter had taught me patience. He understood the capricious behavior of the antelope better than anyone else, and knew how to catch them unaware.

Several of the older cows that watched over the herd had already become restless, manifesting their disquiet by sending out strange guttural warning sounds in our direction. We remained still.

This Lord Derby eland scored a Safari Club International gold medal, Kaga Nze, 1992.

A little water was now rising in the tiny well that Yando had dug. With the help of a leaf rolled up to form a cone, he began to collect the precious liquid that the sandy soil seemed to be yielding reluctantly.

Zoumbala and Pascal had gradually drawn closer and, with studied indifference, were now awaiting their turn, bringing to mind the dignified behavior of the big-game animals when they reach a watering hole after long hours of walking. It was the end of April, a time of year when the Kaga Nze plateau is a furnace. The eland, unlike us, could easily go for days on end without water.

Now the animals seemed more reassured, and the herd, at least fifty head strong, had scattered over an area of several hundred yards in search of the tender young shoots that were budding on branches regenerated by recent bushfires. Three or four of them were large bulls. From time to time we could make out the tips of their horns. Warily, they kept to the center of the herd, surrounded by the cows that shielded them with their bodies. We had been observing them for over a week now and knew there was a great trophy among them. We were certain that sooner or later we would get our chance to claim it.

The sun had already begun its descent toward the horizon, and the blinding glare that flooded this far-away plateau was rapidly fading, giving the illusion that earth and sky were about to merge into one. The fabled antelope seemed to infuse the empty vastness with a prodigious breath of life.

The minutes passed. Michel remained impassive, but I was overcome by the magic of the moment. It called up all kinds of distant, blurred memories, including the dear faces of departed friends mingled with the fleeting shadows of my beloved horses of long ago, thoroughbreds bearing Berber names—Imrad, Tassili, Tarik, Atakor, Tilok, Djahil, La Takouba, Targui, and Hoggar (a gray stallion, the most magnificent of them all).

I was caught up in my reverie, recollecting mad chases on *meharis* in pursuit of the little dorcas gazelles that still inhabit the Tefedest range. I could see them bounding through the tamarisks and the few oleanders that grew poorly in the dried-up bed of Wadi I-n-Amguel as they struggled to escape the Sloughi dogs of the Tuareg. But that was all a very long time ago, on another planet, in the heart of the Hoggar at the very gates to the kingdom of Antinea, the enigmatic queen of Atlantis.

In Michel Kaouche's opinion, the Lord Derby eland and the elephant are the most exciting animals to track. Here, he bows over the neck of one of these magnificent antelope that he loved above all others. He paid his respects in this way to every eland he brought down.

Coming out of my reverie, I realized that the sun, blood-red now as though wounded, was on the point of dropping out of sight. In the distance, the huge antelope filed across a carpet of ash.

"Go on, now's your moment!" The master's voice brought me back to the present. "There, between the two cows—that's the one. Get him!"

I saw the bull's interminable horns raised toward the first evening stars, like a gigantic chimera abroad on the outermost fringe of the universe. The sound made by the impact of the bullet told me the eland was mortally wounded. As though wound on a powerful spring, he leaped up, bucking angrily and kicking out into empty air. Then he staggered, trying to stay upright on limbs that were giving way, and for the first time in my career as a hunter I witnessed in disbelief a most amazing sight (later I would learn that it was not uncommon). Several of the larger females, obviously aware of the weakened state of their old leader, had hurried to his side and were supporting him as best they could in an attempt to keep him on his feet.

And when, inevitably, he fell to his knees and then sank onto his side, they resigned themselves and abandoned him, disappearing unhurriedly into the African night.

Yando approached the dying animal. Respectfully, he threw a handful of the powdery earth into its eyes, where a faint glimmer of life still flickered. When I asked him why, he answered, "I do it so that *bosobo* does not recognize us when we meet him on the other side."

The trackers had lit a large fire. In its light they busied themselves with cutting up the mountain of meat, some pieces of which were already roasting over the glowing embers.

I sat a little apart from the group, observing the almost perfect sphere of the moon through my binocular. On its surface I could distinctly make out small craters that gave the illusion of a thick liquid slowly bubbling. A primitive emotion stirred inside me. I thought of our distant ancestors, those rugged, primeval huntsmen of the early hours of our history, who must have gazed at this same moon, just as I was doing then, and pondered the mysteries of the perilous world in which they lived, their souls fraught with questions to which they had no answers. I felt a kind of tender solidarity with these early men, whom I imagined proudly standing under this same sky and its legions of stars. In a breath, a million years were blown away and it was as though nothing had ever changed on the barren Kaga Nze plateau.

Michel lay back against a tree that had been felled by the wind. As usual, he hadn't uttered a word. All the same, I would have liked to know what was going through his mind.

Kaga Nze Camp, Central African Republic, 1992

In Hemingway's Footsteps

Masai Steppe, Mto Wa Mbu Camp, Northern Tanzania

Tanzania, the lion kingdom at the heart of Africa.

A Farewell to Arms, For Whom the Bell Tolls, The Snows of Kilimanjaro, The Old Man and the Sea, Green Hills of Africa . . . thrilling tales all, and all made a deep impression on the imaginations of the young people of the 1960s. Stories of love and war; hunting, fishing, and bullfighting; of Africa and the Caribbean; of Paris, Madrid, and Ava Gardner! To a young man raring to go, Ernest Hemingway represented the ideal, the ultimate modern adventurer. His style was terse, his novels realistic. He had diced with death to give meaning to life—until that fateful day in 1961 when a shocked world learned that he had taken his life with his own hunting rifle. He had chosen his hour to bow out. I could understand that.

So when, in November 1992, I suggested to my new wife that we begin our life together with a safari in Masailand, I took it as an auspicious omen when it turned out that our route crossed paths with one the author of *Green Hills of Africa* had taken some fifty years earlier. According to the older Masai, our hunting camp was pitched on the very spot where the famous writer had set the stories of his hunts.

As Hemingway put it, "We had come down to the Rift Valley by a sandy red road across a high plateau . . . and into a dusty turn-off that led into a deeply rutted, dust-filled track through bushes to the shade of M'utu-Umbu[1] camp."

My beautiful wife had traveled all over the world but had never before set foot in Black Africa. She was startled in the night when she heard the rasping growl of

---

[1] Known today as Mto Wa Mbu.

"The beast was lying on the mound when three other cats suddenly sprang out from the surrounding bushes."

29

a leopard chasing baboons just above us in the trees overhanging our tents. In the evening she started at the sudden powerful trumpeting of an elephant as it crossed the camp with the light-footed, almost phlegmatic gait peculiar to pachyderms. In the early morning she couldn't believe her eyes when we discovered the footprints of a lion just outside our shower. But what surprised her most was when she caught us setting fire to an ocean of dry grass to chase out the buffalo that were hiding there. To her, we were dangerous pyromaniacs.

But a scarier adventure awaited her. I had shot a lion as it stood on a knoll not far from our truck, where we had left my wife sitting in safety. The beast, which died instantly, was lying on the mound when three other cats, much more impressive than the one I had all too hastily slain, suddenly sprang out from the surrounding bushes. Far from being fearful of our presence, these three were curious and approached their friend, whose body was still twitching. Displaying no hostility, they stood next to the dying lion, some twenty or thirty yards away from us.

My friend Jean-Pierre was with me. Shielded by the trunk of an acacia, we witnessed the rare spectacle without the slightest apprehension. Alas, not so for my poor wife, who was making frantic signs for us to return to the vehicle. But we could not tear ourselves away from this amazing sight and ignored her entreaties, gesticulating back at her mockingly.

Moments later, after the three buddies finally decided to move on, our Kikuyu and Masai trackers set to work loading the dead lion onto the back of our truck.

At that point Kayu, one of the trackers, noticed bees swarming around the truck, attracted by the blood. The bees in these parts are extremely aggressive, and the locals consider them the worst of all scourges. I can still picture Kayu shouting out in panic, "*Hatari*, bees, bees!"

At this outcry our escort scattered, every man for himself. Some just fled as fast as their legs could carry them; others swatted desperately at the air around their heads with branches they had hastily broken off bushes. All this took place under the bemused gaze of my wife, who, quite unaware of the danger, could not comprehend how a team of such experienced hunters, who seemed quite comfortable in the presence of four huge lion, could panic so at the mere sight of what she later called "little flies."

Arusha, Tanzania, November 1992

Dinner in the Bush

Bamingui Camp,
Northern Central African Republic

To Michel Kaouche, who taught me so much.

*A*s usual, the wretched cook had served us the biggest guinea fowl—that is, the toughest! No doubt it was the old cock we had shot the previous day on the banks of the Koukourou. I suspected the cook had spirited away the smaller bird for his own consumption. You really had to keep your eye on the old devil. "But boss," he would say, "I kept the best one for you, the biggest one!" What a hypocrite! For all his airs of faithful devotion, he had an answer for everything and never lost an opportunity to take us for a ride.

It was getting late. Our primitive camp was lit only by the two gas lamps that flickered in front of our modest *boukarous*. A feeble fire was burning itself out a few yards from the makeshift structure that served as our mess hall—a lofty designation for the minuscule straw-covered shed with no floor or walls that our trackers had hastily thrown together with the materials at hand.

From time to time the mournful howl of a hyena would bring us back to reality. We were at the ends of the earth, in northern Central African Republic (formerly Ubangi-Shari), not far from the border with Chad but some five hours from the nearest town worthy of that name. We had no means of communication. As usual, Michel had not bothered to bring along a radio transmitter, as neither he nor I, nor anyone else in our party for that matter, would have known how to use it. So it was best to steer clear of accidents.

In any case, Michel preferred this type of improvised setup, known as a "fly camp," where, he said, we would be spared the "blustering parasites" that hang about most base camps. These braggarts are generally idle, useless youths or aging has-beens who spend their days in a bar, glass in hand, spinning tall tales of hunting exploits or other feats that exist only in their deluded imaginations.

The "old man," Michel, sat across from me. The meager flames that still played on the dying embers would sporadically light up his face, lending the scene a fascinating chiaroscuro quality worthy of a painting by Caravaggio. He was a man of few words and never rushed things. He battled with the rubbery wing on his plate without betraying the slightest irritation. He was not fussy—during forty years in Africa he had seen it all and acquired a good dose of fatalism, that fatalism so characteristic of Africans, who cannot be ruffled, except perhaps by death. And hardly even then.

The tall trees under which we had set up camp almost completely masked the sky and stars, deepening the sense of isolation. From time to time the harrowing, almost human cry of a bushbaby rent the heavy mantle of silence, increasing my rising feeling of oppression.

In those days my sense of entitlement could charitably be put down to youthful ignorance:

"This wine is undrinkable!" I sputtered. Impassive, my companion continued his laborious chewing. And since he was paying me no attention, I went on, "That damned cook has given us the toughest bird of the lot again!"

"Stop whining," he finally grumbled. "It's of no importance. You should have been around in the SAFECA[1] days—we only ever got rice and tinned sardines, and lousy ones at that! And wine? Forget it! You got water from the *mayo*s, filtered if you were lucky. But those were the good old days," he added with a trace of nostalgia in his voice.

At that very moment, as if in agreement with my friend's words, a lion roared in the distance, a long, extraordinary, mighty rumble that shook a listener to the core of his being, awakening every animal instinct.

Michel blinked, his pale eyes flashing in the light of the dying embers, and said, "Did you hear that? What a voice!"

---

[1]SAFECA: A company that organized safaris in Central Africa during the 1970s, for which Michel worked as a professional guide.

He spoke softly, as though afraid of alerting the animal, although it was probably a mile or two away. And then, as though the roaring had been directed specifically at him, his face lit up.

"Just think," he began. "About twenty years ago this part of the Central African Republic was a hunter's paradise. There were vast numbers of animals: thousands of buffalo, antelope, big elephant, and above all I remember huge lion with impressive manes. . . ."

His lips trembled slightly; his right hand went up to smooth his silvery hair, and he carried on speaking: "In the early seventies I had a strange experience a few hours' trek from here. I was guiding two Italians, and we were tracking antelope. We couldn't catch up to them; the heat was unbearable; and our water supply was getting low. The trackers told me we should take a break and try to make it to a watering hole they knew. According to them, it

"At that very moment, a lion roared in the distance."

never dried up. When we finally got there a good two hours later, it was just a muddy hole with a thin trickle of water. A couple of ibis and two or three jabiru storks were diligently guarding it, looking proud.

"The place seemed peaceful enough. It was at the edge of a plateau of reddish laterite that stretched as far as the eye could see. The ever-present water had allowed some sparse vegetation to survive—some high grasses and a few trees were scattered here and there. After the parched terrain we had just crossed, the place looked like an oasis.

"As we approached it, I thought I saw a splendid Lord Derby eland heading for the water, like us. I looked around quickly and spotted a thick bush growing under a parasol acacia. I immediately ordered the team to take cover in it while we waited for the antelope."

The old hunter paused for a few moments, gazing into space, or into the past. He drank some wine, grimaced, and whispered as though reliving the scene, "Time passed. We huddled together and waited for the antelope. It didn't reappear. Had it picked up our scent? I didn't think so—we were downwind. That's when a large buffalo with magnificent horns suddenly came out of the bush. It was obviously thirsty too, and looking for water. Steadily and silently, head down, it made its way confidently to the watering hole.

"My Italians, of course, immediately made as if to shoulder their powerful guns, but I signaled to them to wait. Why wasn't the antelope coming? I would have much preferred to have them shoot a prestigious antelope rather than a buffalo, no matter how handsome."

At that point in the story, from the highest branches of the trees bordering our camp, we suddenly heard the war cry of a leopard—a most peculiar sound like the grating of a saw being rubbed back and forth through hard wood: *Rrraaa . . . rrraaa.* The baboons in the trees around us instantly went mad, unleashing a torrent of invective at the cat. Like a weary schoolmaster tired of lecturing unruly pupils, Michel patiently waited for the ruckus to die down.

"As I was saying," he continued, "it wasn't the antelope but a buffalo that appeared, and I had a hard time keeping the guys from blowing its brains out. It had no idea we were there and made an easy target. A good thing, though, that I made them hold their fire, because, to our surprise, an enormous lion loomed up out of the grass, where it had probably been lying in wait for hours.

It pounced on the bull. To our amazement, we saw the buffalo, unfazed and sure of its strength, stand its ground and fight off the predator, which slunk back into the bush whence it had come—or at least that's what we thought. So that was why the antelope had turned around! Its keen sense of smell had detected that cat. . . ."

Michel looked at me with that roguish air he sometimes displayed when secretly savoring his own misadventures, calling me to witness: "You know something about animals, but you're not going to believe this! The buffalo was sure it had scared off the intruder and so made its way to the water and began to drink. That's the very moment the crafty lion chose to bound out of its cover to attack the unsuspecting buffalo a second time. The bull valiantly dodged the lion and ran after it, bellowing like crazy, horns down, ready to gore it. The lion panicked and didn't know which way to turn. And then it finally leaped right into the tree we were hiding under!"

Ah, how the old adventurer's face, generally so stern, beamed as he recalled that extraordinary scene! He chuckled into his graying beard, lifted his head, and, departing from his usual reserve, added coarsely, "You can imagine the looks on the faces of those Italians.

"They were paralyzed with fear. There they were with that four-hundred-pound cat perched right above their heads with its tail dangling only a few feet from their noses, and more than a thousand pounds of beast snorting and pawing the ground not a stone's throw away. It only lasted a few minutes, but were they ever long! By now the buffalo was desperately thirsty and went back to the water to drink. The lion was more cautious now, after what had just happened. It seized the opportunity to drop quickly from its perch and disappear into the grass, so terrified by the whole experience that it hadn't even detected our presence."

"But why didn't you shoot the lion?" I asked.

He shrugged, thought it over for a bit, and answered on a more serious note, "It was a maneless lion, a poor trophy. Shaky as they were, those guys would probably have missed it or, worse, wounded it," he muttered disgustedly.

At that, he got up from the table, bade me good night, and went off slowly to his *boukarou*.

Another roar, closer than the first, thundered through the night. It was a powerful sound that silenced all the other sounds of the bush. Michel had

"The buffalo stood its ground and fought off the predator."

taught me that a big lion, when in hunting mode, would roar out every fifteen or twenty minutes. Which was exactly the amount of time it had taken him to recount the funniest story I had ever heard. And coming from him, I knew it to be completely true.

Northern Central African Republic, April 1993

On the Banks of the Faro River

Northern Cameroon

When the gods want to punish you, they answer your prayers.

Karen Blixen

On February of 1994, Michel suggested we meet up in northern Cameroon, a region he knew well, having once spent ten years or so there. Cameroon, which extends from Lake Chad in the north to the borders of the Congo and Gabon in the south, was a French protectorate from 1916 to 1960, when, like most of the former French colonies in Africa, it gained its independence. Presidents Ahidjo and Biya governed wisely, preserving solid ties of friendship with France, thereby helping the new state develop in relative prosperity.

Cameroon, more than seven hundred and fifty miles long on a north-south axis, is a miniature representation of practically all of Africa. Its geographical location provides an exceptional variety of resources, not only of flora and fauna but also of populations[1] and traditions.

In the north, on the border with Niger, are the semi-desert regions of the Sahel, peopled by ethnic groups of Sudanese origin: The Tupuri, Massa, Bororo, Hausa, Choa, and Fulbe, all of whom can be recognized by their delicate features and proud bearing. The farther north one goes in sub-Saharan Africa the

---

[1]Cameroon is said to have more than two hundred ethnic groups.

A beautiful, young northern Cameroonian girl with a superb Murano bead necklace.

41

comelier and more statuesque the people, as if the beauty of the faces were in deliberate contrast to the aridity of the landscape.

The nomadic lifestyle of these shepherds seems to have saved them, for the time being at least, from the decadence that has corrupted sedentary populations. With the horizon as their only border, they have colonized vast territories, some groups having pushed beyond the tenth parallel into the valley of the Nile, following the river back to its sources to reach the Great Lakes region (the Tutsis) and as far as the Rift Valley (the Masai).

In the west and the south live many thriving tribes of Bantu stock with their more rough-hewn features. These are the Tikar, Duala, Bassa, Bamun, and especially the Bamileke, well known for their talent for business and commerce.

And last come the mischievous Pygmies, those matchless, gnomelike hunters who live scattered deep in the forest not far from the equator, along the borders with Congo and Gabon, out of the way of the civilized world they mistrust.

In the north of the country, between Garoua and Ngaoundere on the banks of the Faro River, I discovered an exceptionally beautiful, captivating region to which I would return again and again with undiminished enthusiasm. The following incident took place there.

Less than an hour of darkness remained when a man traveling on foot approached our camp, already lit by the first flames of the fires our trackers had rekindled in front of their modest huts. The visitor appeared very frightened and told us that he had been sleeping out in the bush a few kilometers away when he was rudely awakened by the angry roaring of several lion.

After listening to his story, we set off in search of the big cats without even taking the time to finish breakfast—the Africans say that hunters should never eat their fill because hunger sharpens the senses. We found them easily because, unlike us, they were sated, having feasted on an old roan antelope that had fallen into their clutches. They had already devoured the entrails and the tip of the muzzle, their favorite morsels.

There were three of them, basking tranquilly in the first rays of sunshine. They lay not far from their catch, watching over it to dissuade the hyenas, vultures, and other inferior predators from coming too close.

I decided to take the handsomest of the trio. It was an easy shot, and the bullet lodged in the animal's chest, killing him on the spot. To this day I'm not

The whole team poses proudly with the dead baroga. *The death of a lion, their hereditary enemy, is a big event. The trackers, waiters, porters, driver, cook, gardener, and skinner are all there, striking a formal pose. Each would try to filch a bit of skin, a bone, or, if they were really daring, a claw, a precious talisman that they would keep forever.*

sure why I did it. As Michel pointed out—albeit too late—it was by no means an exceptional trophy.

The Africans weren't concerned by such considerations. As usual, they demonstrated their happiness with the hunt, singing and dancing around the remains of the unfortunate *baroga*.

The carcass of the lion had been hoisted onto a bed of foliage on the back of the truck and we were driving back toward camp when we were stopped by a man who was evidently having trouble with his ancient motorbike. Seated on the back was a passenger, a young woman whose great beauty struck me instantly.

A protracted discussion in Fulfulde immediately ensued between the members of our group and the hapless motorcyclist. According to Haman, a tracker, the man was the "Reverend Pastor" of Gamba, on his way to a neighboring village to help conduct an important ceremony, accompanied by his daughter.

The girl was elegantly dressed in the costume of the women of the north. Michel, down-to-earth as always, drew my attention to the superb glass bead she wore around her neck. It was one of those conical beads with a blue-and-white herringbone pattern that the glassblowers of Murano had begun making in the seventeenth century. Such beads were used until very recently as currency by the Portuguese, the Dutch, and the traffickers of all stripes who did business with the natives of these remote regions.

Feeling slightly awkward, I pointed to the precious jewel and requested that Haman ask the worthy clergyman if he would consent to part with it. To soften the man up, I added that I myself had a beautiful young daughter of the same age as his own.

With hardly a moment's hesitation, the good reverend set a price for the transaction so steep it did away with any misgivings I might have had. He wanted forty thousand CFA francs[2], no less, which in those days in northern Cameroon represented a small fortune.

Somewhat taken aback by the high figure, I made a counter-offer through our faithful interpreter of half the sum requested. This time the man thought it over for a bit and then, pointing at the lion whose back was just visible through the foliage covering it, said that he would accept my price on condition that I throw in one of the large claws from the lion's front paws.

I was well aware that most Africans see such claws as priceless and attribute to them unlimited supernatural and even therapeutic powers. Therefore, despite the protests of the whole group, who deemed such a high price unacceptable, I agreed. To clinch the deal, I handed over two ten-thousand-franc notes to the shrewd clergyman on the spot, and even invited him to visit our taxidermist at camp as soon as possible to collect the promised claw in full payment, once the lion had been skinned.

And then, at a sign from her venerable father, the young girl promptly came forward and with graceful agility climbed onto the back of our vehicle, slipping

---

[2]The CFA franc is the currency of the African Financial Community, and 40,000 CFAs were the equivalent of approximately U.S. $80.

On the banks of the Faro River.

docilely between the dead lion and the indifferent trackers. To my immense embarrassment, I realized that as a result of an absurd misunderstanding, I had just become the proud owner of one of the loveliest young women in all of northern Cameroon!

Koti Manga, Cameroon, February 1994

Tembo's Revenge

Omay Camp, Zimbabwe

Killing is not a feeling that you share. . . .

Ernest Hemingway
Green Hills of Africa

On the third day in Omay Camp we killed a fine sable antelope in the hills bordering Lake Kariba. Russel Tarr, the professional hunter in charge of the safari, told us that it was the biggest trophy shoot he had ever set up in his entire career. He measured the annulated, scimitar-shaped horns several times and was visibly delighted.

Over the next few days we searched fruitlessly for ivory-carrying elephant. Frustration began to set in, but then, just as night was falling on the tenth day, we finally crossed paths with an old bull with magnificent tusks. The left one was chipped, however, and this made me hesitate.

Because the safari was nearing its end and large elephant were few and far between, Russel insisted that I shoot the animal, which was making its way along the sandy bed of a wadi. We followed it, walking along the embankment high above the dried-up river and keeping ourselves well hidden in the vegetation.

Shooting an elephant is not the same as shooting your common warthog. I had to drop it with one clean shot. I'd long anticipated this moment and remembered my mentor's advice: "Between the eye and the ear; closer to the ear than to the eye."

It was as if I'd cut the strings of a giant gray cardboard puppet. The elephant collapsed in a heap as though disjointed, dead before he even hit the sand, which flew up in a dusty cloud.

"Good shot, sir, good shot!" Russel exulted.

He was even happier than I was.

It was now almost completely dark and we had to get back to camp. We left one of the two Matabele behind to keep the hyenas away and watch over the ivory.

At the crack of dawn the following day we were ready to get down to work. Already, though we were far from the villages, we could see long lines of men and women rushing in, having been informed of the kill through the amazingly efficient "bush telegraph." Some carried large jute sacks folded under an arm; others balanced heavy calabashes on their heads.

The women set to work with the fiercest determination. Half naked, often with a newborn strapped to their backs, they plunged straight into the foul-smelling carcass, hacking furiously at the mass of meat with their rudimentary knives, defending their share of the loot like lionesses and threatening each other with blood-smeared blades.

In no time, all that remained of what had once been a marvel of nature was a shapeless, decaying, shredded heap. The scene gave me pause. The fact that the elephant's tusks weighed about fifty pounds each no longer mattered to me. The plain truth was that I had destroyed a magnificent creature that was about fifty years old—my age, maybe even older. This animal had probably been born during World War II and wandered freely ever since from one end of southern Africa to the other. It had escaped the poachers' traps, the ivory traffickers' greed, and the relentless pursuit of tribes driven by their insatiable hunger for meat. And then its path had crossed mine, and there its life had ended. Fate?

One day my turn will come. Would that my departure could be as momentous!

I decided to call off the safari. Now that we had killed the elephant, it seemed inconceivable to hunt anything else. Before flying back to Victoria Falls, I invited the whole team to a farewell party at a small lodge a few miles from camp. As we were getting into the ancient Land Rover, Russel remarked that my rifle would just be in the way and that it would be far better to leave it behind at the camp. I yielded, albeit reluctantly.

My wife sat up front with Russel. I sat with the trackers on the open platform at the back, along with the game scout that the wildlife department had imposed on us. The game scout was a civil servant who escorted us everywhere we went,

Sable antelope (Hippotragus niger) *that earned a gold medal from Safari Club International.*

"I was horrified to see an elephant charging toward us."

somewhat against our will. It was his privilege, owing to his high status, to carry his service weapon, a rifle so antiquated it looked unworthy of even a fairground shooting stand.

Our road dipped into a hollow, at the bottom of which snaked a river that still held some water. Our guide drove his rattling old heap down into it, and the car crawled forward, its passage obstructed by rocks and other protrusions.

Suddenly, from the bush came a strident trumpeting. I turned around and was horrified to see an elephant charging furiously toward us, as if fully aware of our precarious position. Its ears were flapping like the wings of a giant butterfly, and already its tusks bashed at the Land Rover, which by now was stuck in the rocks at the bottom of the ford. Through the window that separated us, I caught my wife's worried look as she watched from her seat next to the driver, who was intent on extricating us from the infernal trap in which we were caught. We all knew that the elephant could tip the truck over like a mere toy, and I bitterly regretted having been persuaded by my friend to leave my .375 H&H behind.

That's when the despised game scout, whom we had all been doing our best to ignore, jammed the barrel of his old peashooter against the forehead of the colossus, whose trunk was now flailing over our heads.

A feeble shot rang out. The stunned elephant staggered drunkenly, hesitated a moment, then turned on its heels and disappeared into the forest, scattering droplets of blood in its wake. I was still quite dazed when one of the Matabele, who had quickly recovered his wits, looked at me and proclaimed in broken English, "It *tembo* revenge, sir!"

Although I am not in the least superstitious, I must confess that I promised myself then and there that I would never hunt elephant again.

Victoria Falls, Zimbabwe, March 1995

An Invaluable Network

Northern Cameroon

One of them even tried to sell us a terracotta necklace that he claimed dated back to the "age of the dinosaurs," no less!

*B*efore he became a professional hunting guide, Michel had spent some fifteen years as a school inspector. In this capacity he had covered almost the whole length and breadth of Chad and Cameroon, visiting each village with a school and going deep into the remotest areas. When he went on inspection tours in the south, it meant paddling in a dugout, escorted by his Bassa aides, up the Wouri River to the heart of the equatorial forest. Out west, in Bamileke country, he trundled around in an old van; elsewhere, for lack of practicable roads, he traveled on horseback, by bicycle, and even on foot when necessary.

Driven by a great passion for hunting, he took the opportunity afforded him by these tours to hunt leopard, lion, and elephant, all of which proliferated in those halcyon days. Many of the Africans who had attended the public schools established by the French colonists remembered this singular teacher with a mixture of respect and admiration. There was not a single village in the whole of Cameroon where almost everyone didn't immediately recognize and welcome him like a friend.

In the course of his peregrinations Michel had acquired a rare knowledge of the art and culture of the main ethnic groups, and in many cases had even learned to speak their language. And if he had long since hung up his guns, it was done purely to make better use of his time hunting for ancient artifacts of artistic interest.

Allergic as he was to bureaucracy, Michel paid little attention to the exacting rules that new administrations surreptitiously introduced over the years, more

"The eland bull stood out in copper silhouette against the fiery horizon."

to fleece antique lovers than to protect a cultural heritage for which the corrupt civil servants hardly gave a fig anyway.

After each safari, we would always spend a few hours hunting for antiques in the handicrafts markets of the large towns—Ouagadougou, Cotonou, Garoua, Bangui, Douala, N'Djamena—where everyone knew Michel. Some of the self-styled "antique dealers" had been his pupils—brilliant ones, of course—which was useful when it came to doing business.

That year we had shot an old lion and a fine roan antelope (*Hippotragus equinus*) with white face markings and annulated, saberlike horns. One evening, after tracking a herd of eland all day, we caught up with it shortly before sundown, as often happens. A large bull attended by his cows, one of which appeared receptive to his advances, was nibbling delicately at shoots of false gardenia while courting his mate. He stood out in copper silhouette against the fiery horizon, forcing me to squint as the majestic animals wandered back and forth across the disc of the sun, which was rapidly disappearing.

Moved by the beauty of the scene, I exchanged a glance with my friend Michel and refrained from shooting, leaving the regal antelope to his tender lovemaking. Taking care not to spook the herd, we turned back under the reproachful gaze of Yando and Zoumbala, for whom this meant a loss of half a ton of excellent meat.

I made no excuses: Africans know that there are days when the lion pay no attention to the gazelle that come to graze among them with total impunity. In any case, night was falling quickly and it was better to give up than to risk wounding such an animal for the sole benefit of the hyenas and vultures.

Jokingly, I told Michel, "We'll spend the money we've just saved on taxes at the handicrafts market in Garoua."

He smiled back. My reasoning, though to his mind badly flawed, appealed to him. He would often remind me of it later, on those days when we seemed jinxed . . . it was a joker to fall back on when our luck was out.

At hunt's end we headed for the handicrafts market, passing first through the *gri-gri* market. From that place emanated, despite a burner in which some incense sticks were smoldering, the stench of poorly tanned hides, badly cleaned bones, and viscous body fluids collected from the putrid carcasses of various animals, right down to the most repulsive creatures such as toads, reptiles, and

Old Choa woman in the handicrafts market in Garoua, northern Cameroon.

carrion eaters—all of which the sinister African apothecaries used to concoct the most disgusting pharmacopoeia.

The handicrafts market was an indescribable clutter: Glass beads from India, necklaces of false Venetian pearls, fabrics "Made in Holland," wooden masks of imitation ebony, crude copies of Benin bronzes, all of them heaped together in grimy little stalls whose owners swarmed around us like a cloud of melipona bees over a herd of buffalo. One of them even tried to sell us a terracotta necklace that he claimed dated back to the "age of the dinosaurs," no less!

Among the bric-a-brac in an old Choa woman's shop, buried under a tangle of carnelian bead necklaces, yellow amber rosaries, and multicolored glass pendants, we unearthed two ivory bracelets that were obviously genuine. The "white gold" from which they were carved glowed with a deep sheen. It was hard and dense with soft, pinkish reflections, indicating that it had been carved from a block of ivory cut from the center of an old forest elephant's tusk. Time had

crazed the surface of the bracelets with fine bluish veins like those that dapple the breasts of the buxom Flemish women so dear to Rubens.

Hanging from the old woman's gnarled fingers, the bracelets formed two almost perfect ellipses, slightly worn in those places where repeated everyday gestures had left their mark. These bracelets bore witness to the past of an entire continent, and to Michel and me they meant more than the very best of game trophies.

After lengthy haggling and with much patience, a cardinal virtue of the Africans, we managed to persuade the old woman to part with them for several thousand CFA francs[1].

Our protracted negotiations done, we set off for the Garoua airport to catch a plane to Douala, the country's economic capital. When we arrived, the airport was a veritable oven. The air conditioning had broken down several years earlier, and, without it, a bouquet of indefinable odors—the sour reek of sweat mingling with stale tobacco—and a range of other unwholesome smells wafted throughout the place.

Although there were no more than two or three flights per day, the town had built an airport of disproportionate size for its domestic traffic. It teemed with people and was permanently besieged by hordes of jobless, penniless idlers on the lookout for naive travelers from whom to extort a few cents in return for some minor service.

On the filthy floor a group of poor wretches, including some miserable legless cripples, begged halfheartedly for alms that were rarely forthcoming from passersby indifferent to their fate. Opposite us, three scantily clad prostitutes sat in a line on a bench attempting to catch the attention of waiting passengers. One of them, her thighs conspicuously spread, sent us languorous looks that were meant to be enticing but came across more as a plea for help than as an erotic invitation. Her emaciated face was little more than skin and bone, her cheekbones jutted out, and she stared at us with feverish eyes that left little doubt about the illness that was consuming her. Now and again she forced a smile that revealed her few remaining teeth, yellowed by cannabis. She could hardly have

[1]One thousand CFA francs is approximately two U.S. dollars (2009).

57

been more than twenty and probably knew that the AIDS virus that infected 75 percent of the region's prostitutes had already got the better of her.

As usual, an unjustifiable plethora of surveillance and maintenance staff were employed to look after the place. Most of them sprawled about shamelessly, while others prowled around the vast hall in search of newcomers to swindle under some pretext or other.

It was the beginning of a scorching afternoon, and the passengers for the flight to Douala were ready to embark. A motley band of noisy, gesticulating people lined up under the watchful eyes of two imperturbable customs agents, stiff and awkward in threadbare uniforms spruced up with handsome butter-colored gloves. There were very few whites.

When our turn came, the two watchdogs, who had seemed quite placid up to that point, suddenly sprang to life and ordered us to open our hand luggage, in which they promptly discovered the bracelets we had purchased only a few hours earlier. Negotiations ensued, "African style," that brought us to the brink of an apoplectic fit. The pig-headed officials' sole purpose was to extract a substantial amount of baksheesh from us, on the pretext that we were unable to provide a proper receipt stating the origin and nature of our precious purchases. I could hardly imagine the old Choa woman, who could probably neither read nor write—though she could certainly count!—drawing up such a document.

Our explanations met with the same mind-numbing responses, over and over again:

"Where's the receipt?"

"You must show the receipt."

"You'll have to pay the fine."

Behind us the crowd was growing and a few travelers were becoming impatient. We were at a stalemate.

Trying to find a quick way around the situation, I made things worse by foolishly remarking that I had most likely left the receipt in my suitcase, knowing that our luggage had already been loaded into the hold of the plane that was sitting out in the blazing sun on the tarmac. I was astounded when the officials immediately dispatched a team to recover the case, which was buried under tons of such assorted parcels as only the Africans can lug around with them when they travel.

Michel continued to refuse, on principle, to pay out a single cent. Things were not looking good at all, especially as the arrival of my suitcase had been announced, heralding a humiliating and ruinous defeat for us.

Suddenly, I saw Michel push through the surrounding crowd, which, worryingly, was starting to show signs of hostility. He chased after a soldier in fatigues who was walking confidently down the main corridor. He hailed him like an old friend: "Hey, (I didn't catch the name)! Remember me?"

Clearly, he had recognized one of his old students.

Astonished, the fellow, who looked like a security guard because of the fat revolver slung on his belt, stopped, acknowledged Michel with a wide grin, nodded, and was about to reply but my friend, confident now, broke him off:

"What the hell are you doing in this damned airport? If you have any authority here, could you please tell these two s.o.b.s to let us leave?"

Finally having a chance to get a word in, and still smiling broadly, the man answered, "Of course, Papa Kaouche, how could I forget you?"

"So what do you do in this miserable airport?"

"I am the minister of Defense, Papa Kaouche—at your service, sir!"

A few minutes later we sailed through customs, heads high, amid angry looks from all the other passengers, who were not about to forgive us for the two-hour delay these ridiculous formalities had caused.

Garoua, northern Cameroon, February 1996

Friends

Northern Cameroon

The wind had taken away my friends.
And now it was blowing at my door.

Rutebeuf

*L*ion often travel in pairs as they roam the vast, empty expanses of western Africa. In a hostile environment where the pickings are slim, they form strong bonds that increase their chances of survival.

That year, we spotted the tracks of two large males and had been following them for almost a week without catching so much as a glimpse of the animals. Even so, we were aware of their every move. Indeed, when trackers in these parts of Africa find the spoor of the larger game in the dust of the trails, they are able to rapidly deduce a host of information about the identity and behavior of the animals that have left the subtle clues. In the case of lion, the trackers can tell us their number, their sex and size, how fast they are traveling, and whether they are on the prowl or have just feasted and are taking a postprandial stroll. Yando and Zoumbala could read the ground and tell whether an animal had managed or failed to capture a warthog, a hartebeest, or a roan antelope. This skill transformed the hunt into a captivating game of strategy.

And then, one morning just before full daylight, the two large cats bounded out before us, crossing the trail we were following as we searched for the night's tracks. Driven by an almost mechanical reflex, I quickly squeezed off a bullet that seemed to hit its target, and in the half-light a shadowy figure appeared that seemed to be moving like a wounded animal. Zoumbala and Yando excitedly urged me to take

"The valiant animal refused to abandon his comrade."

another shot. I was reluctant, however, because, although killing one lion in these circumstances would be a victory for us, killing two was unthinkable.

My finger on the trigger, I knew—because I had almost paid for the lesson with my life a few years before—that it was very risky to let a wounded lion escape into the bush. Torn between the near certainty that my aim had been true and the insistent urgings of the trackers, who were afraid that they might have to engage in a dangerous pursuit, I made ready to shoot again.

Michel kept his calm, as usual, and firmly dissuaded me.

Emboldened by the rapidly brightening daylight and with infinite precaution, we were finally able to get near. Greeting us was the sight of one of the protagonists lying in the grass, well and truly dead, with the other by his side, like a sphinx guarding the doors to an ancient temple.

In spite of all our efforts to chase him off, the valiant animal refused to abandon his comrade, apparently overcoming the fear that we most certainly inspired in him. He could not bring himself to leave, seeming unwilling to give his friend up for dead. When much later he finally did, he went off reluctantly but not without giving us a look so dark and full of reproach that I have never forgotten it. It was a look that was almost human.

That night, a loud, plaintive howling rent the silence. It went on until dawn and then stopped. I never heard it again, except in my memory. From time to time it haunts me still.

Gamba, Cameroon, 1997

Hunting the Baboon

A Battue, African-Style
Cameroon

*I'd like to try to write something about the country and
the animals and what it's like to someone who knows nothing about it.*

Ernest Hemingway
Green Hills of Africa

For some time now, the trackers seemed to be up to something. On several occasions I'd intercepted furtive exchanges, secretive confabulations, and this was completely unlike them—the locals were not given to plotting and planning, preferring to live in the present.

The previous evening they had returned from the village of Gamba with dogs—mangy, shifty-looking yellow curs. One must admit that the surly animals have good reason to be unsociable. A dog's existence in Cameroon, as in the rest of Africa, is a far cry from the gilded existence led by our own thoroughly spoiled four-legged friends. Tolerated only for as long as they serve some purpose, they wander around the towns scavenging for food, knowing that at the slightest misdemeanor they themselves will wind up in the pot.

One evening I had noticed Adamou at the door of his *boukarou*, busy sharpening a rudimentary spear, its haft tarnished by the sweat of his hands. Using a conical stone, he was beating out the rusted piece of metal that formed the blade of his protohistoric weapon.

Intrigued by these strange preparations, my curiosity got the better of me. I found an excuse to talk about it with Haman, who was generally regarded as a

"The younger Durus were pelting the unfortunate creature with pebbles."

figure of authority among our staff. I was quite surprised when he told me, with characteristic restraint, that "at the request of the Gamba authorities" they were getting ready to organize a battue, or beat, for baboons.

I was aware that the Duru, though they did not readily admit it, were very partial to the meat of the yellow baboon (also known as the cynocephalus or dog-head monkey) and indeed preferred it to any other.

Though the trackers were not overly keen on the idea, I invited myself along on the expedition and, the following day, joined the small group that broke camp at dawn. The team consisted of our own trackers plus half-a-dozen newcomers who were obviously delighted to be included in the operation. Some of them, clearly the older Sara, had front teeth that were hideously filed into swallowtails, reminding me very much of the terrifying features sported by cannibal warriors until not so long ago.

The dogs were restrained by leashes fashioned from the fresh bark of a silk-cotton tree, one of those majestic trees that often grow in the center of the villages. The natives slice off the bark just like the Mediterranean cork growers do. In addition to the aforementioned spears, my African friends carried heavy clubs, their inseparable machetes, and a bow or two.

Along the way, I noticed the younger members of the party picking up pebbles from the beds of the *mayo*s we crossed.

It took us two long hours of walking to reach the foothills of a volcanic plateau that I was familiar with because I had hunted eland there a few months earlier. As we climbed the escarpment, the column split up into smaller units, each taking a different direction. They stayed in contact with each other through a system of discreet calls that blended with the early morning sounds of the bush, which echoed with hundreds of different animal cries.

The plateau had been chosen because it was fairly wide, but its main advantage was that it was only lightly wooded with only a few kapok trees scattered here and there, survivors of the many bush fires. This, as I understood later, was essential to the success of the plan.

The locals, who were very motivated and inventive when it came to hunting for themselves, knew that many herds of baboon took this route on their way to drink at Mayo Alim, which flowed a little to the west of the high plain. Indeed, we didn't have to wait long before we saw several of the animals emerge cautiously from the high grass bordering the woods. They first looked around carefully and then stepped out into the open. The young males led the way, followed by the females, some with babies clinging to their bellies or backs. (The position depends on the age of the babies: The youngest spend a few weeks latched to their mother's breast before moving up to the next level.)

Well-guarded in the middle of the group, a big old male the size of a small lion suddenly appeared and resolutely stepped out onto the arid plain, apparently causing the locals to decide that it was time to act. They loosed their dogs and rushed out from their cover after them, making a hellish din that caused the baboons to flee in all directions in sheer panic. Some, thinking this was the way to safety, quickly climbed into the branches of the nearest tree, which was exactly what the beaters were hoping they would do. In one perfectly orchestrated movement, the men formed a circle around the tree in which the unlucky old baboon thought he had found safe haven.

I must admit that at this stage of the proceedings I could not figure out how our guys were going to go about dislodging the big *baba* from his comfortable perch in a fork more than ten meters (about thirty feet) off the ground. As things turned out, I was in for quite a show!

The dogs circled the kapok tree, barking madly and leaping up against the trunk to incredible heights. The younger Duru, almost as frenzied as their dogs, were pelting the unfortunate creature hard with the pebbles they had collected for this very purpose. They occasionally managed to hit the animal, which reacted by baring its powerful canines. Some just shouted and brandished their clubs, while others, meaner, used their spears to launch flaming bundles of dry grass at the creature. The rest of them shot at it ineffectually with their bows and arrows—a nightmarish scene.

All at once, at a sign from Moussa, a Sara tracker, the assailants leashed their dogs and pretended to back off. Moussa made a show of grabbing a machete and then approached the tree alone. By now the prisoner was huddled, terrified, in the top branches. Cleverly, Moussa mimed the actions of a woodcutter and pretended to chop down the tree, which of course he had no intention of doing—it would have been far too great a task. But the tracker knew exactly what he was about. His pantomime had an immediate effect on the primate, which, misled by its own intelligence, believed the kapok tree would soon be felled, bringing

"*In no time at all, Adamou and Haman gathered up dry grass and lit a fire, onto which they threw the still-warm carcass. . . .*"

him down with it. Moussa kept up the performance, and the baboon, somehow reassured by the fact that the man was alone, slid quickly from branch to branch down to the ground . . . right into the midst of the Duru, who had been waiting for this fatal mistake. Setting the dogs loose, they rushed in for the kill.

Though brief, the ensuing fray was indescribable. When it was all over, the dogs were tied up again. Some were bleeding profusely, though it was hard to say whether their wounds had been caused by the sharp canines of the victim or, more likely, by the clumsy spear work of their masters, who in any case were evidently unconcerned.

In no time at all, Adamou and Haman gathered up dry grass and lit a fire, onto which they threw the still-warm carcass. A pleasant aroma of charred meat soon spread around the crackling fire.

The purification done, Adamou extracted the remains of the tortured victim from the fire. The baboon was unrecognizable without its fur, its skin smooth and its stiff limbs comically spread. It rather resembled a toad on its back, penis erect.

Showing no respect for the dead animal, Adamou made an incision in the skin of the belly, taking great care not to puncture the intestines, which, dilated from the heat, pushed out of the abdomen like the crown of a large, pearly cauliflower. Then, rather obscenely, Moussa impaled the smoking carcass on the end of his spear, hoisted it onto his shoulder, and, with a gleeful shout, set out on the road back to camp. I was speechless.

It so happened that another surprise awaited me that morning. Lost in my thoughts about the barbarity I had just witnessed, I was making my way back to camp, some six miles away, with Umaru, a tracker, when I felt drops falling on my shoulders. At first I thought it was raining. Looking closer, I was nonplussed to see that it was not water that was raining down but blood, which was splattered all over the ground.

Umaru pointed upward, and there I saw two buffalo that had been killed by poachers, cut into strips, and strung in the branches above us like bloody garlands of biltong. While my Africans had been murdering a baboon by luring it into a kapok tree, just a few hundred yards away others had been massacring buffalo and hanging them out to dry.

Ah, Africa!

Properly, you should know that our safari comrades hunt only for meat; hunting to acquire a beautiful or rare trophy is a concept that is foreign to them. I have often observed the bemusement of our trackers, who watched us, curious, as we painstakingly measured the exact length of the horns of the antelope we had shot. At times Zoumbala, the most facetious of them, had even ventured comments such as, "The horns for the whites, the meat for us," which told a great deal about what he thought of us.

The Africans will eat just about any animal, including some very unlikely ones, such as monitor lizards and even pythons. They have no qualms about capturing them by sticking their children down the snake holes, where the huge reptiles coil themselves tightly around the youngsters' legs. Both "bait" and snake can then easily be extracted together.

This python is almost five yards long. Although not poisonous, the python is a formidable adversary that can strangle its prey in a matter of seconds or break a limb with a snap of its tail. After a half-hour battle, Amadou finally got the better of this one using only his bare hands.

I've seem them tucking into agoutis, the large, unappetizing rats that you find all over Africa, and giant bats. Porcupines, tortoises, anteaters (aardvarks and pangolins), the mongoose—nothing is safe from these insatiable meat eaters.

The butchering of the large animals such as elephant, hippo, buffalo, and eland is almost a ritual. Every part is used according to precise rules, leaving hardly anything to the carrion-eaters. A few clean bones are all the vultures and hyenas will get. Even the parts we would consider unfit to eat, such as the entrails, genitals, spleen, and skin, are carefully removed.

In certain areas even the big cats sometimes fall victim to this compulsive need for meat, and end up as the daily fare of certain tribes. Though the lion and panther are considered inedible because of fetishistic beliefs, they often end up as ingredients in medicinal concoctions with alleged therapeutic powers.

In countries with a large Muslim population, the entire pig family (Suidae)—warthog, bushpig, and giant forest hog—generally escapes the stewpot, being protected by the Koran, which prohibits the faithful from any contact with pigs.

Apart from these, the only other creatures that are scorned by our African friends and do not end up in the pot, as far as I know, are the Mustelidae—civet, honey badger—and some of the canines, including jackal and hyena. But I would not bet on it.

In the bush, news of the capture of a large animal spreads like wildfire. Very often, the "authorities," greedy civil servants, are attracted like vultures and claim their share, often helping themselves generously before anyone else. What remains is then distributed according to criteria that have always escaped me. It is not rare for one member of a team (very often the "foreigner"—i.e., someone from the city, such as the driver) to have to make do with a portion so small it would fit in the palm of a hand, whereas others, for no obvious reason, might be allotted a whole quarter of the animal.

A fifteen-hundred-pound buffalo or eland carcass can disappear within a few hours. Some pieces are sent to the families back in the villages many miles away. At other times, the meat is discreetly sold, making its way onto restaurant menus in nearby cities. One thing is for sure: Nothing is wasted.

On days of plenty the huts are festooned with strips of meat dripping blood. Hanging on long ropes strung between the trees, the strips give off a putrid stench as they dry in the sun, crusted with purplish flies.

Sometimes, smoking tables are hastily set up. I have memories of baboons roasting slowly, their faces contorted, their hands clenched, in poses that would make your flesh crawl. And it's no use pointing out (I have tried) that these primates are our cousins. You only receive dark, hostile stares devoid of any compassion.

In Africa, *nyama* is a serious matter.

Douala, Cameroon, 1998

How to Hunt a Warthog

Northern Selous, Tanzania

Here I am, and here I stay.

*MacMahon, nineteenth-century president
of the French Republic*

Toward the end of an afternoon, Marcel, our hunting guide, who had eyes like a hawk, urged me to go for a long shot—something you should never do—at what he judged to be a "big" warthog. The adjective referred to the size of its tusks, which would make a fine trophy. Somewhat reluctantly, I fired.

"Got him!" Marcel announced.

I wasn't so sure: "You think so?"

"Yeah, you got him. Let's go see!"

With the whole group behind us, we made for the place where the animal had supposedly been hit. Blood! The large red stains on the ground seemed to bear Marcel out.

"I think he took it in the right leg," Marcel declared.

Right or left, it was all the same to me. I had a feeling the animal was going to get away, especially as night was falling. We were about to abandon the chase when Marcel pointed out the entrance to a deep tunnel that had been dug in the sandy soil by an aardvark, the weird anteater that the Creator, evidently at a loss for inspiration that day, patched together from the front of a pig, the ears of a donkey, and the hindquarters of a kangaroo.

A few drops of blood, already dried by the hot wind blowing over the Mjeta plain, showed us that the animal had indeed been squatting in the aardvark's

His teammates hauled the little man out along with the warthog.

lair. If Marcel was to be believed, the warthog, an ugly 170-pound pig with tusks as long as fifteen inches, had backed into the dark den and was waiting for us, solidly entrenched.

The trackers, game for anything as always, tried to flush it out by using long wooden sticks they had cut from nearby bushes, but, hardly surprisingly, they were getting nowhere. After a bit, Marcel ordered them to stop their fruitless poking and go gather some dry wood. "As much as possible," he added.

The men understood what our hunting guide had in mind. Given their characteristic enthusiasm for this sort of task, they had lit a fire in the opening within a few minutes and were throwing burning embers down into the hole.

But in spite of these drastic measures, the warthog stayed underground. It was getting late. The hole was smoking like a volcano, and Marcel instructed the men to block up the opening with branches, declaring that we would come back as early as possible the next morning.

At dawn we were ready to set to work. The team was the same but for the addition of a newcomer, who stood out because of his small stature and cheerful demeanor. This little fellow, who wore a sort of Basque beret that he

Marcel Tiran and his hunting party.

never took off, as though it offered some protection, immediately cleared out the opening of the anteater's long tunnel, slid nimbly into it, and disappeared completely from view.

I feared the worst, expecting to see him reappear at any moment astride the warthog's angry snout. Marcel was amused at my fears and reassured me, "No need to worry—if the pig isn't already dead from its wound, it'll have suffocated by now."

The white soles of the intrepid spelunker's shoes wiggled. It was the signal his teammates had been waiting for. They grabbed hold of him and tugged with all their might, hauling him out along with the warthog, whose tusks he was gripping tightly as he might the handlebars of a racing bike. Once back in the open air, he announced, laughing heartily, "It's rightly roasted, sir!"

Dar es Salaam, Tanzania, September 1998

Eland of
the Bad Moon

Northern Cameroon

For our unforgettable trackers:
Zoumbala, Yando, Adamou, Moussa,
Issa, Oumarou, Haman, and all the others.

*A*s U.S. President Bill Clinton, backed by all "civilized nations," prepared to launch Operation Determined Force, which was going to bury Serbia under a hail of bombs, I was once again making preparations to meet Michel in northern Cameroon in yet another attempt to track down the elusive Lord Derby eland.

The safari began well. Thanks to our tracker Zoumbala and his unrivaled talent for precisely imitating the call of the lion, we soon managed to run to ground a sizable old cat.

But then came a bad moon.

Yando was first to point it out on our return from hunting one evening. As he looked up anxiously at the ill omen, now in its last quarter, he made no secret of the fact that it was a bad sign. In Africa, celestial warnings are taken seriously, especially when a persistent harmattan wind is blowing down from the desert regions in the northeast, clouding the atmosphere with fine pink, sandy particles, creating a surreal and rather oppressive haze.

Despite our forebodings, we were about to encounter the Lord Derby eland, those giant antelope that appear just as suddenly as they vanish into thin air. It happened one morning at dawn as we arrived at a high plain to which the animals had been drawn by the tempting and tender young shoots of the Isoberlinia bush.

The large, awe-inspiring bulls kept to the center of the herd surrounded by the vigilant cows that guarded them. The herd, around fifty head strong, was moving along sedately, a halo of morning mist adding an enchanting, poetic note. Because the eland were downwind from us, they picked up our scent immediately and fled as one, moving off at a full trot.

Then began a lengthy search that kept us hard on their trail for days on end, dawn till dusk, across the arid slopes of volcanic hills and through bushland still smoking from recent fires. More than once, we thought we wouldn't have the strength to go on. We burned in the sun and suffered from a raging, unquenchable thirst, having to ration the last tepid drops of water at the bottom of our canteens. The trackers themselves, usually so restrained, threw themselves on brackish ponds from which even wild animals were reluctant to drink. Sometimes, using their machetes, they dug like elephant do in the damp sand of the *mayo*s to collect a little murky liquid that they gulped down gratefully.

As for the eland, they eluded us again and again. Whenever we thought we had a chance of intercepting them, they easily evaded us. Dispirited and powerless, we could only watch as the long cohort of elegant silhouettes gradually withdrew into the distance, hill after hill. From afar, with their immensely long horns, they looked like a blessing of small unicorns traveling on to another world.

And then one day, when we had been foiled yet again and given up all hope, one of these majestic antelope stood before us almost defiantly, as near now as it had previously been distant and inaccessible. Automatically, I hoisted my rifle and sighted on the boldly exposed flank of this finest of the large bulls. Nothing could save him now.

However, when the shot rang out—it still echoes in my memory—the animal did not fall to the ground as expected but glanced at us condescendingly and unhurriedly returned to his place in the herd, which galloped off in a cloud of dust. Zoumbala was the first to realize that the bullet had shattered against the trunk of a frail shrub growing in its path.

"A few months later, in the same place and with the same team, we actually shot the 'eland c

moon' without much difficulty." The animal earned an SCI gold medal.

Astonished, I heard Yando mumble resignedly, "It is the curse of the bad moon, boss."

We did not see the giant eland again on that hunt. True to legend, they had vanished just as they had appeared.

A few months later, in the same place and with the same team, we actually shot the "eland of the bad moon" without much difficulty. I do not remember where exactly the star of ill omen was sitting in the skies at the time, but clearly the bad spell had been broken.

Garoua, Cameroon, February 1999

The Kudu of Mount Gorongoza

Mozambique:
Nhacainga Camp, Chimoio Region

An intense inner life suffices unto itself;
it could melt twenty years' worth of icefield.
Louis-Ferdinand Céline
Journey to the End of the Night

In 1975 Mozambique, a former Portuguese colony that had only just gained its independence, and then only by resorting to armed force, became embroiled in a civil war that would last for twenty years. When the rival FRELIMO and RENAMO factions were not busy killing each other, they were massacring the wild animals that had once been so abundant in Mozambique, originally one of the best-stocked countries in southern Africa. When the opposing forces made peace in 1994, one of the first tasks of the so-called government of reconciliation was to try to rebuild big-game hunting, as many of the neighboring countries had done, which just goes to show that on this continent, hunting and peace are intricately linked.

A few years later, my friend Jean-Pierre and I were among the first to head off there. In September 1999 we stepped off the plane into a country that had been laid to waste. Devastation was everywhere, and the people were living in appalling poverty.

In a bid to feed their armies, both sides had exterminated elephant and buffalo as well as eland and other antelope without the slightest compunction about making free use of the weapons—even the helicopters—that the Soviets and the Chinese had so generously supplied to the opposing forces.

Our host, whom I will call Bill, was a famous professional hunter and former mercenary. He recounted how, around the barracks of the revolutionary forces, he had occasionally come across piles of bones, grisly remnants of elephant and buffalo and even of the combatants themselves.

Bill looked much as I imagined a Nazi panzer division commander might look. He had gray-blue eyes, a steely gaze, and an Aryan hide weathered by the African sun. In spite of his highly precarious situation, he had never lost his very British affability.

Before winding up in this "graveyard," this veteran of internecine conflicts had at one time hired out his services to the Rhodesians in their struggle against the ZAPU (a Zambia-based liberation guerrilla group), as well as to Amin Dada, the bloodthirsty Ugandan dictator, who at the time had been having some trouble with a recalcitrant opposition. Bill was persona non grata in most of the neighboring countries and had no choice but to make a permanent home at his hunting camp, alone with his devoted companion Elke, a German woman he had seduced and stolen from her husband during a safari several years earlier.

On some nights, over a drink, he would unburden himself of his ignominious past, confessing to the murder of thousands of elephant and a good number of rebels on behalf of his unsavory employers.

As for Elke, though she never said as much, it was plain that she now regretted having let herself be trapped by the handsome adventurer. Though she bore her situation with dignity, I suspected that deep down she was apprehensive about the future. The day of our departure, as we were all making our good-byes, she climbed up beside us in the Land Rover and called out, in a timid attempt at humor, "Good-bye, Bill!" Getting no reaction, she quickly hopped down to resume her place at the side of her valiant warrior, who was too thick-skinned for such feminine subtlety.

Elke cooked day and night. She was aware of the shortcomings of the area as far as hunting went and did her best to make our stay as pleasant as she could. There was absolutely no doubt that here was a real lady who had washed up on inhospitable shores. I often wonder what became of her.

Much to our surprise, in the area of the reserve to which we'd been granted access, only the kudu had survived in any numbers. This was unexpected and probably due to the kudu's suitability to life in mountainous regions, to the fact that they can go for days without water, and no doubt also to the disappearance of their natural predators: lion, hyena, and leopard.

Early one morning, however, as we made our way along a trail, a herd of Cape eland suddenly came into view, as if conjured up, on a deserted plateau that had recently burned over. The huge herd appeared directly in front of us, indifferent to our presence. Wisps of ashy dust swirled up by the wind lent a surreal air to the scene. Several hundred of the animals stood almost immobile, statuelike. Among them, the silhouettes of large bulls stood out. The eland were packed together tightly like a Roman legion massed for an assault, and seemed to be waiting for a signal of some kind to continue their journey toward some far-off promised land. Their taupe-colored coats blended into the grayness of their surroundings, conferring an ethereal lightness to this extraordinary gathering. It seemed that all the eland of Mozambique were massed on this strip of land. The trackers were mesmerized.

The Cape eland, unlike its Central African cousin, is of only minor interest to hunters. So we left this biblical procession to its enigmatic pilgrimage. Strangely,

An exceptional greater kudu, Mozambique, 1999.

we didn't see those animals during the following days, or even cross their path again. The antelope had vanished as though they had never been there at all, except in our imaginations.

Back at camp in the evening, when we told Bill (who had already had a few) of our amazing encounter, he did not seem at all surprised. Like a frustrated prophet at long last vindicated by a tangible sign from the heavens, he told us that these prodigious animals were but the frontrunners in a great comeback of the fauna of old times. He had always firmly believed that the lion would return first, followed before long by many other species returning to reclaim their territories. He got quite carried away and went on to say that in the early 1900s there had been so many buffalo in the southern African savanna that they formed herds several thousand head strong. The large beasts left behind them such desolation that those who brought up the rear dropped like flies for lack of food, to the benefit of the lion and other predators, which could consume but a fraction of the carcasses that lay rotting in the sun. To Bill's mind, life would one day return to the way it had once been.

We said nothing to dampen his optimism. It would have been unkind to silence the last faint notes of hope that sang in his heart, the fragile illusion that kept him from a one-way journey into despair.

The war of independence was over and illegal hunting was rife. The region was infested with poachers, who set nasty traps with steel jaws made from suspension springs they salvaged from the wrecks of vehicles left behind by the militias of both sides.

We were aware of the dangers here. To avoid being caught ourselves in one of these infernal torture traps, we were careful to let our trackers, themselves former FRELIMO or RENAMO fighters, scout the terrain before we went near the watering holes. To top it off, we also had to watch out for the antipersonnel mines that were causing so many ghastly mutilations among the unfortunate population.

The large kudu remained unapproachable, especially the old bulls whose soaring, twisting horns represented such fabulous trophies. They kept giving us the slip, hiding in the rocky *korongos* and escaping at full gallop the instant they detected our presence, setting off rockslides that echoed from hillside to hillside as if mocking our efforts.

Late one afternoon, worn out by much fruitless clambering over hillsides under the blazing sun, I shouted, "Jean-Pierre, I'm beat—to hell with your damned kudu!"

"Quit complaining," came his reply. "Just think of all the poor people stuck in the rush-hour traffic back home."

Ah, how right he is! I thought to myself as I contemplated the sun going down in a lilac sky, setting the peaks of Mount Gorongoza ablaze.

Pretoria, South Africa, 1999

Paka Doumé– The Well-Named

Selous Game Reserve, Tanzania

I was the richest man in the world. Gold was my ruin.

Blaise Cendrars

Of all the game reserves in Africa, Selous is where you will find the greatest concentration of big game roaming free. Local legend has it that if the whole world were to become a desert one day, it would be here, on the banks of the Rufiji River, that the very last man and the last antelope would engage in the final face-off.

The most magnificent reserve in all of Africa is named after the legendary English explorer, Frederick Courteney Selous. A gold prospector, professional hunter[1], builder of railroads, and military hero, he was one of the great nineteenth-century adventurers, along with the Livingstones and the Stanleys of this world. Having joined the British army as an officer with the Royal Fusiliers, he went out to Africa and was killed in action at the age of sixty-five in southern Tanganyika, modern-day Tanzania. He was laid to rest at the foot of Mount Hatumbala, close to the Rufiji River, in the same spot where he met his sudden death.

Selous Game Reserve, a World Heritage site, is managed jointly by the World Wildlife Fund and the local authorities, who have realized that big-game hunting,

---

[1] F. C. Selous (1851–1917) was Theodore Roosevelt's guide during Roosevelt's hunting expedition in East Africa in the early twentieth century.

Tracker Paka Doumé perches atop the heavily laden Land Cruiser.

if practiced ethically and fairly, does not endanger wildlife but is an essential factor in its management and protection. In places where there is no longer any hunting, the noblest species will die out, never to return.

The western limit of the Selous is marked by the Luwegu River, which flows in the Mbarika Mountains a few days' trek southwest of Dar es Salaam. The Luwegu is a river like no other I have ever seen. It is very wide but shallow, and its banks and bed are covered with fine sand the color of raw cotton, such as one finds on the beaches of the Indian Ocean not so very far away. It wends its way, like molten crystal, through vast expanses of timbered hills. Protected by cliffs too steep to climb, and far from any human presence, it brought to my mind the primeval river of a lost paradise.

We pitched our camp on the sun-baked bank by the Luwegu's gently lapping, limpid water. Barely visible, the camp blended into the surrounding vegetation like a Sudanese poachers' den. The *korongos*, dried-out, sandy stream beds that surrounded us on all sides, threatened to break some vital part of the old Land Cruiser at any moment or even tip it over. The refrigerator we carried with us had not stood up to the journey, forcing us to dump the cheese that I had taken so much trouble to bring with me from Switzerland.

In addition to Tadé, the driver who was to save us from disaster on innumerable occasions, the staff at the camp comprised a totally incompetent waiter such as Africa will sometimes produce, a shifty-looking cook who couldn't even fry an egg, some jobbers (a mechanic, a skinner, and a few bearers) who were equally useless, and finally a single tracker known as Paka Doumé. This was ironic because *paka doumé* is Swahili for male cat, and we had thought this poor devil was blind when he jumped into the car on the first day, peering at us with eyes that were almost opaque[2]. In spite of this he wore a constant smile, baring huge, bright, white teeth.

I had serious doubts about the man's abilities, which I must admit was neither charitable nor sympathetic of me. But in my defense I should point out that an African tracker's reason for living is to hunt antelope and track lion,

[2]Paka Doumé was probably suffering from an illness called river blindness (onchocerciasis) that is transmitted by a small fly. When it bites, it deposits a small worm whose parasitic larvae enter the eye and lead to total blindness.

so some irony, be it in poor taste, was not entirely out of order. Although it was evident that his eyesight was far from keen, the "male cat" did appear to command a certain respect from the pack of losers who otherwise constituted our hunting company.

Despite our housekeeping problems, it was a magical, even dreamlike, place. We half expected Tarzan to appear at any moment, heralded by his jungle call. The reserve teemed with life: elephant, hippo, waterbuck, and a host of other animals, and birds too, especially waterbirds. The jungle feel was enhanced by a small, swampy lake not far from our camp, with foul-smelling, muddy water that swarmed with crocodile and hippo by the hundreds. Day and night, the latter, tightly bunched together, snorted angrily at us as soon as they sensed our presence.

The Matabele of the Zambezi say that the hippopotamus was the last of the African mammals that God created. He used whatever was left over, which in their eyes accounted for the hippo's ugliness and cantankerous disposition.

Already several times, when we had made as if to approach these hulking animals, one of them—no doubt an old bull—had immediately charged, causing a wave of panic in our small group. One day, I was even forced to make a one-hundred-yard dash—which I didn't know I was still capable of—with my rifle under my arm. It was then that I finally made up my mind to get the hippo that threatened to kill us every time we came near.

My friend Jean-Pierre had dubbed the place the Cauldron of Death—for good reason. In addition to the delightful neighbors I have mentioned, the bush also harbored thousands of buffalo. One evening I counted three hundred and fifty of them in a single herd as they crossed our path on their way to an evil-looking, stagnant pond where they were in the habit of drinking.

The elephant that hung around our small canvas lodge paid no attention to us. It was clear they felt they were on their own turf and that we were unwelcome intruders, to be treated with indifference and reserve.

But no matter! We were there to hunt *chui,* the leopard, a cat so discreet as to be almost invisible, a creature that was at home in the rock crevices and dense *bakos*. We had discovered some prints in the sand down by the water.

To attract and catch a *chui* we had to lure it with bait, which we hung from the branches of specific trees, selected according to a set of very complicated

Waterbuck killed on the Luwegu River.

criteria—on which, you may well guess, Paka Doumé was the authority. In the course of three weeks we baited almost a score of trees in all, hanging impala, gnu, hartebeest, and even kudu.

Each morning we would check the bait, traveling over miles of rough track, through sand that trapped us for hours, and along the top of steep, treacherous cliffs that offered such impressive views across the bush that all danger was forgotten. It was beginning to look as if we were going to get to the last day of the safari without striking luck—not a single leopard had shown the slightest interest in the choice morsels we were offering, not even the kudu!

I was weary and discouraged. Ill-kept and with a three-week beard, I looked like an escaped convict. I was ready to throw in the towel. Only scrawny Paka Doumé, who one day actually covered almost forty miles on foot through the mountains to join us, all the while carrying a radio transmitter on his head, still seemed to believe in our lucky star. Here were Job and Tobias combined in a single black man.

And so it happened that one morning as the expedition was drawing to a close, after we'd made the rounds of all the baits except for two trees, I took the opportunity to hop off the Land Cruiser as we passed close to camp. I told the others I was going to pack my bags while they went to check on our last two baits, though I didn't pin much hope on them. Our departure for Dar was set for the next day at dawn.

Less than an hour later, while passing my tent on his return, Jean-Pierre called to me in an offhand tone of voice: "Come on, Eddy, this is no time for sleeping—there's work to be done. Someone paid our bait a visit during the night."

At first I thought it was a poor attempt at a joke, though that wouldn't have been like my friend. He quickly went on, "Don't get your hopes up, though. I saw the pugmarks in the mud—a medium-size print, probably a large female. But you never know."

You have to remember that in big-game hunting it is strictly forbidden to shoot the females, whatever the species. If we did, it would put an end to our hunting. Naturally, it fell to Paka Doumé to direct the construction of the *boma*, the blind that is set some distance from the bait, in which we were going to hide in hope that at dusk the big cat would deign to come and finish its meal. The *boma* had to blend into the surroundings, be located downwind, be neither too far from nor too close to the bait and yet away from the path that we supposed the leopard would take, and so on. This was a job for Paka Doumé and his band of merry men.

The preparation of the final phase of a leopard hunt is similar to the night before a battle, when everyone gets ready to play his part. The hunter readies his weapon, testing its accuracy, adjusting the sights, checking the ammunition, etc.

Once holed up in the *boma*, not a movement, not a sound is allowed. The wait can last for hours and can seem like an eternity!

By midafternoon we were at our post. Through a small opening we could keep an eye on the leg of hartebeest in an advanced state of decomposition that hung from the tree like a ham from the ceiling of a country kitchen. Given that we were downwind, now and again the stench of carrion wafted our way. Senses keen, we waited in silence, motionless.

The hours passed, punctuated by the sounds of the bush: the songs of the many birds—some of them very strange, like the calls of the hornbills and the francolins—and the sounds of the cicadas and the toads, which provided the high and low notes of the orchestra. With nightfall came the maniacal laugh of the hyena that had picked up the smell of rotting meat given off by our trap.

Close to the equator, the African night comes abruptly. The sudden darkness is like the blackness that cloaks a thick-curtained room when the flame of an oil lamp or a candle dies out.

We exchanged looks heavy with resignation. It was plain that we were going to have to throw in the towel. By then, only the feeble light of the last-quarter moon still enabled us to make out the branch we expected the *chui* to climb.

Suddenly, as if by some conjuring trick, mirage, or hallucination—as though projected by a magic lantern—the dark, phantasmagorical silhouette of a big male cat appeared, standing tall and taut as a bow. He stared suspiciously at our straw blind, apparently unable to remember having seen it before. Inside we hardly dared breathe. The slightest movement, the slightest sound would jeopardize everything.

Effortlessly, with one deft movement of a front paw, the cat scooped up the antelope haunch and set it neatly on the branch from which it had been hanging. After a last quick glance in our direction, he finally made up his mind and began to devour it greedily. Through the scope of the .375 H&H I could make out the animal tearing at his prey against the background of clouds and stars.

A loud crack rang out in the night, frightening some herons and guinea fowl that squawked in surprise. A heavy body thudded to the ground. Death had struck a killer. Unfairly? I don't know. Killing had been in the animal's nature. In its own lifetime it had meted out death without any of the qualms and soul-searching that beset us contradictory humans.

High over the bed of the Luwegu, a flock of white egrets flew silently above us, like the mechanical shadow of a ship cutting through the boundless starry sky. A shooting star bearing a message of hope shot across the firmament as if to sow the Milky Way with its cosmic pollen.

Back at the camp, it was party time. Paka Doumé and his friends drank and sang and danced around the campfire. The firelight flickered on the carcass of the poor *chui* they'd hung from the fork of an acacia, in the African manner. For

"I could make out the animal tearing at his prey against the background of clouds and stars."

them, this was as good as it got! For my part, I fought against a tide of sadness and thought of my loved ones back home.

That evening the well-named Paka Doumé, who was almost blind and had no money to his name and no future, was the happiest man in the world.

Dar es Salaam, Tanzania, 23 September 2000

The Lion of the Doukoua

Northern Cameroon

When you are back over there in Europe,
and you feel your heart beating faster,
you will know Zoumbala is thinking of you.

Zoumbala

It was getting late and the heat was already almost unbearable when we reached the small coomb (narrow valley) on the mountainside to which the pursuit of the three lion had led us. The small valley, source of the Mayo Doukoua, seemed like paradise after the vast, desolate plains, blackened by ash from recent bush fires, that we had crossed before reaching this unexpected oasis.

Zoumbala had discovered a huge python and was teasing it with a stick. I was amazed at how motionless the reptile remained, no doubt believing itself protected by its almost perfect camouflage. He finally left the snake in peace, and we talked.

In the course of our conversation he asked me whether my wife had been pleased with the many trophies from previous safaris that I had supposedly taken back as gifts for her. I explained that white women much preferred jewelry to skins, even lion skins.

The Banda tribesman was taken aback and looked at me uncomprehendingly. Clearly, it was quite inconceivable for him that a hunter's wife might not be rapt with admiration for—or, better yet, totally in awe of—a husband who had brought her so many lion skins. He put an end to the conversation by promising

"It was getting late and the heat was already almost unbearable."

to write[1] to her and resolutely popped into his mouth the kola nut he had been preparing during our interesting little chat.

For Zoumbala and his comrades, scoring a lion skin would be a dream come true, comparable to Jason and the Argonauts' conquest of the Golden Fleece. Michel, on the other hand, seated on a bed of leaves, was firmly grounded in reality. He had opened a nasty-looking tin of sardines and was scraping out the last few bits of fish with an ancient horn-handled knife he told me had been his father's.

"You know," he said, spreading the last oily scraps of his unappetizing meal on a dry crust of moldering bread, "I can see you settling down somewhere around here with three or four wives, your children, and your cattle, far from your stock exchange, your money, and all that financial bulls--t you're always worrying about."

---

[1]See Zoumbala's letter at the end of this chapter.

"Less than an hour of daylight remained when Zoumbala rested the bell of his huge trumpet

on top of a giant mushroom-shaped termite nest."

In spite of his bantering tone, deep down I had to admit that the colorful picture he painted was not without appeal.

Having said his piece, he stashed the precious knife safely away in the pocket of his field jacket and squeezed some lemon juice into a filthy cup, adding a little tepid water from a metal flask that must have dated back to the Great War (his grandfather had fought the Germans at Verdun). He drank it down slowly and then signaled that it was time to make our way back.

Feeling a bit disappointed, I took a moment to dip my face into the cool water of the river and then, resigned, took up my place again in the small group that was already making its way down the southern slope of Mount Doukoua.

Zoumbala headed the column, my heavy rifle across his right shoulder. The Banda was a tall man, well built and athletic, and had a certain elegance about him that was unusual in the men of these Central African tribes. He lived from hand to mouth, collecting wild bee honey and fishing or hunting along the Bamingui River as the spirit and the seasons moved him. He sought the company of women, no matter if they were loose women, and got drunk on palm wine.

His soul was untainted by the poison of ambition, and he wandered free across the wide, open spaces of Africa just as his ancestors had done from time immemorial. I am sure that is why I liked him more than all the others. Besides, a strong, tacit bond had existed between us ever since the day I had very nearly died in his arms after being attacked by a lion that had been wounded by a clumsy hunter.

That had been more than ten years before, in the *bako*s of the wild Youhamba River, north of Ubangi-Shari. At the time of that dramatic incident, when it was time for me to leave for home, and knowing that correspondence between us would be impossible, he said something to me I will never forget: "When you are back over there in Europe, and you feel your heart beating faster, you will know Zoumbala is thinking of you."

We had been tracking for around ten days already and had come to know our adversaries well. Three different sets of tracks were visible on the trail. One of them was more deeply etched in the ground than the others and belonged without a doubt to the leader of the group. It was his skin we were after.

Life was not easy for the large predators on these vast, arid plains, and their never-ending quest for what fresh prey there was forced them to cover huge distances, both day and night. For Michel and his trackers, interpreting the

"He came close enough for me to make out the malachite green pupils in his topaz yellow eyes."

tangle of signs in the dust of the savanna was an art, and although we could not see the cats, we knew their every move and felt quite certain that sooner or later they would make a mistake that would allow us to catch them.

Michel led his safari with a high hand and did not confer much. When he did, on rare occasions, ask for our opinion in a difficult situation, it was only to point up our lack of perspicacity, often with a touch of humor. We accepted this with good grace because we well knew that he was one of the best professional hunters in the whole of West Africa.

Certain evenings around the fire, over a glass of scotch, he would tell the most incredible stories of his experiences thirty or forty years earlier, when these remote regions still formed part of France's huge colonial empire. I had heard all of his stories many, many times over in the ten years I had been hunting with him, but the storytelling was still magical as he told us how he had relieved a gang of Duru poachers of the horn of a black rhinoceros, or how he had single-handedly chased off five or six Bororo tribesmen and confiscated the tusks of an elephant they had just killed.

With his gray hair and a beard à la Hemingway, Michel had the soul of a Charlie Marlow, Joseph Conrad's brooding, nostalgic hero. To look at him, you could not help thinking that he was living out the last chapters of his own personal legend as he pursued these lion, which were dying out and with which, I had come to realize, he identified a little.

A few years before, we had shot a big old lion, scarred and skinny. We had lured it to its death through Zoumbala's talent for imitating the roar of a lion, using his own version of a call made out of sheet metal and animal hide. As morning broke, the unfortunate animal, believing he was answering the call of another lion, had rushed headlong into the death trap we had set for him. When it came to luring big game, Zoumbala was matchless in the whole of central Africa.

I can still picture Michel, bent over the body of the lion and stroking it. Far from exulting, he had declared tersely, for my benefit, "Shame we can't bring him back to life!"

Herein lay the contradiction in this adventurer: For many years he had traded in ivory, skins, and all kinds of trophies; now he showed affection for the magnificent creatures he had stalked so relentlessly from the savanna of northern Chad to the forests south of the Ubangi.

Less than an hour of daylight remained when Zoumbala rested the bell of his huge trumpet on top of a giant mushroom-shaped termite nest. Hidden in a leafy bush, he watched for a signal from "the boss," who stood leaning nonchalantly against the trunk of an acacia, his arms behind him.

When Michel gave the signal, a quick nod, the Banda blew a long, deep roar on his archaic instrument, immediately setting off hysterical screaming from the frightened baboons playing in the branches close-by. Almost at once, a threatening echo answered us from the thick *bako* near which we were posted. The lion were there, and already moving in our direction.

Zoumbala continued to call them, and the cats replied in turn with vindictive growls, all the more nerve-wracking as they came closer and closer. The most combative of the three shot out of the thick vegetation ahead of the others. With his raised tail lashing the air angrily, he came close enough for me to make out the malachite green pupils in his topaz yellow eyes. His two younger pages, more cautious, hung back, but they too stared intently at us.

Michel was totally impassive and appeared impervious to the poetry of the charming tableau. He had not even picked up his rifle, which remained propped close to his side in the fork of a thorn tree. Behind me I felt the trackers' excitement. I knew that they too were spellbound by the sight of these fascinating creatures.

Ready to fire, I drew a bead on the animal's coppery flank. The lion seemed to hesitate, indecisive about his next move. At that moment those three lion spoke to me of the very essence of the miracle of life on this earth, whatever its origin. In the rapidly fading evening light, the three silhouettes looked as if they had stepped straight out of an early Renaissance painting.

I was perfectly aware that the slightest pressure of my forefinger would imprint a bloody wound on the very spot marked by the cross hairs—the seal of death—and destroy the golden icon held prisoner in my lens. I could not bring myself to fire. I recalled the words of the French poet Alfred de Vigny, who wrote in his *Death of the Wolf:*

> I rested my head on my powderless gun
> Lost in reflection, unable to fire.

A breath of wind stirred the air. Slowly, like a mirage fading, the three shadows disappeared in the heat haze of dusk.

Without comment, Michel and his team set off to walk back to camp. As for me, knowing I was out of earshot of them, I found myself mumbling, "This time, it won't be necessary to resuscitate him."

Suddenly, a roar rumbled down from the nearby hills, bathed in the early light of the last-quarter moon, and tore through the silence that had settled on the plain. Then came the retort of a second lion, nearer this time, rolling like a wave over the volcanic plateau across which we were hurrying.

A shiver ran through me. My companion had already disappeared into the twilight, and I had to hasten my steps to follow him in the darkness, through the heart of the bush.

Garoua, Cameroon, February 2002

Zoumbala's Letter

Zoumbala Michel | le 21-8-2002
Pisteur safari
Cameroun et
Centrafrique. Baningui   Chère Madame Eddy

J'ai le grand plaisir de vous faire une notte.
Vraiment, Madame. Avant, tout, Je donne une bonne Santé, et,
je vous souhaite bonne année.
Je demande, Est ce que tout les safaris que le Patron vient
faire, ici en Afrique. Vous avez lui fait un cadeau ?
Ce, n'ais pas pour rien que, j'ai demandé. Parce que, lui,
Cet un chasseur agrégée, un tireur de la grande ligue Ennemi
des lions. Je l'aime beaucoup, je priais le Dieu, qu'il
le garde dans toutes les conditions. Ton mari là, il est
très intelligent.
S'il vous plait, Madame, Je vous empris de bien vouloir
lui faire une honneur très favorable, et, très important
il n'as pas d'autre comme d'autre chasseur.
Voici la raison pour là quel, je vous envoie cette notte
à propos de mon Patron unique. Que, vous pouvez
lui faire son cadeau des lions.

Amitié

Translation

21 August 2002

Dear Mrs. Eddy,

I am very pleased to write this note to you. Truly, Madam.
First of all, I wish you a good health and a good year.
I am asking: For all the safaris the boss makes here in Africa, did you give him a gift? I am not asking this without reason, because he is a master hunter, a highest class shooter, the enemy of the lion. I love him very much and I pray God to protect him in all situations. Your husband is very intelligent man.
Please Madam, I beg you to honor him very favorably, and, very important, he is not like other hunter.
For this reason, I am sending you this note about my unique boss so that you offer him a gift in thankfulness for all the lion skins he brings you.

Your friend.

Mister Mrosso, A Good Man in Africa

The Masai Steppe, Tanzania

Please, sir, I would need another zebra.
Mister Mrosso

Ten years had passed since our previous visit, and we were back again at Mto Wa Mbu on the banks of Lake Manyara in northern Tanzania. Our camp, clinging to a mountainside, overlooked the grandiose Rift Valley, which runs like a gigantic tribal scar down the left cheek of Africa. Its Olduvai Gorge is said to be the cradle of mankind. From there we had an uninterrupted view of the Masai Steppe, sunburned and parched from several months of severe drought.

There were more Masai than ever, roaming tirelessly over scrubland overgrazed and worn bare by their innumerable herds. Trees and bushes were becoming scarcer by the day. Every now and again one would see morani, young Masai warriors, gathered in small groups under umbrella trees. Only the women and children were at work, tending huge herds of emaciated cattle, sheep, and goats.

Still, we were pleasantly surprised to see quite a few Grant gazelle and graceful Thomson gazelle, impala, zebra, and gnu. They appeared to be cohabiting in perfect harmony with their domesticated brethren. Their presence in such large numbers was due to the proximity of the Tarangire and Ngorongoro Crater reserves, veritable treasures of nature. Here the Engaruka Valley channels the wandering animals as they migrate toward the banks of Lake Natron and the

The author's wife, Maria Dolores, is shown with a lesser kudu—an SCI bronze medal winner—on the Masai Steppe. The lesser kudu is a localized, shy antelope that favors the dense, dry thornbush thickets of the Horn of Africa, in hilly or mountainous regions. This graceful animal is one of the most-sought by connoisseurs of African trophies.

pasture lands of Amboseli National Park. Like milestones in the sky, the sacred peaks of Ol Doinyo (Mountain of God), Lolmalasin, and the Olmoti Crater keep watch over this earthly paradise.

Of the staff from the previous year's expedition to the banks of the Luwegu River, only the faithful Tadé had come along this time. He was joined by the usual waiters, porters, drivers, cooks, and skinners, who all had very specific jobs. One man was the "water heater," whose sole function was to produce sufficient hot water for the comfort of the guests, a job he carried out in such a manner that I found it almost impossible to synchronize my daily ablutions—even a short shower—with his own timing. No matter: The water heater was unfailingly civil whenever we encountered him, an empty plastic mineral-water bottle in hand, the symbol of his high office.

But he was not the most colorful member of our hunting party. The key man (just as Paka Doumé had been on our previous safari) turned out to be our game scout, a sort of official game warden: Mister Mrosso.

This worthy representative of the Tanzanian authorities didn't really look the part. A game scout's mission is to enforce hunting regulations, and you therefore might expect him to have a Rambolike physique. But ours was quite the opposite. Mrosso was a puny fellow with an expressive face and a pensive, almost paranoid look about him, which is uncommon among Africans. As a badge of office he wore a beret that he pulled right down to his ears. It was red when he was on

duty, but he turned it and wore it green side out on off-duty days, in a sort of peaceable ecological allegory. In full regalia, this black Woody Allenish figure disappeared almost entirely inside his faded khaki tunic—possibly once the top half of a uniform that had manifestly not been made to measure.

Mrosso was an odd, meek-looking character who walked with short, quick steps and hunched over, almost hopping along like the jumping hare, a small African kangaroolike rodent that lived around our camp.

From the first moment on, however, Mrosso wielded an almost shamanic influence over our group that was to lead us, as you will read below, to the outermost bounds of hunting ethics.

Before long, on the pretext of an order from on high, he politely requested that we procure for him, without delay, a gnu and a Grant gazelle. The two animals were destined for the municipal authorities of Mto Wa Mbu, who apparently were hosting the prime minister of the United Republic of Tanzania on an official visit.

The higher interests of the country were at stake, so we promptly carried out the order, feeling almost honored to have been designated for such a mission. Meanwhile, by the time the game had been taken and delivered, we had lost a whole day.

Delivering the meat was not just a matter of handing it over to any presidential banqueting department; rather, we brought the gazelle discreetly to the garbage-strewn courtyard of a dilapidated house in one of the sorriest neighborhoods of Mto Wa Mbu village. But Mister Mrosso presided over the operation with such contagious serenity that we were not fazed in the least.

Within the vast perimeter designated for our hunt was a village called Selela that we had to cross several times a day. Even if one had tried, one would have been hard put to build anything more unsightly than this little town. Set on a desert hillside, Selela was a collection of dwellings devoid of any African style or tradition. The houses, built of crooked wooden poles and grayish stones and roofed with grimy metal sheeting, were scattered here and there higgledy-piggledy at the whim of the local "architects." The looks of the place were of absolutely no consequence to the motley, idle population that shared the alleys of the shantytown with the goats and donkeys that rummaged for food through the garbage littering the ground.

Nailed to the eaves of one of these miserable shacks was a wooden cross, indicating to the lost traveler that here was a place of worship. On the many occasions he passed by the place, Mister Mrosso doffed his cap, crossed himself, and prayed, the precious beret clutched to his chest between his joined hands. Sometimes we would use a route that took us right around the church, thereby to keep the cross in view a bit longer, allowing our pious friend to prolong his contemplation.

But for Mister Mrosso, routine incantations alone were not sufficient, and he used the power his lofty position conferred on him to assist his less fortunate brethren. Sometimes he would have our Toyota stop to pick up schoolchildren as they dallied on their way to the primary school in Selela. They often came from quite far away, and he would admonish them for their repeated tardiness. On other occasions we would pick up poor women exhausted by their heavy loads, who often had an infant strapped to their backs.

One day we even had to cut short the hunt to rush an ancient Masai to the hospital in Mto Wa Mbu, escorted by his entire, very worried family. According to Mister Mrosso, the patriarch was suffering from a disorder of the spleen. Who were we to question Mister Mrosso's diagnosis?

And thus our time was divided between hunting and charitable missions, under the leadership of our game scout, who was gradually emerging as our spiritual guide. It is only fair to acknowledge that Mister Mrosso never failed to praise us for our noble conduct. On occasions when he was feeling especially benevolent, he would even grace us with a solemn "God bless you, sir."

Though Mister Mrosso's duty, as I have already pointed out, was to protect the wild animals rather than the population at large, he was not one to forget the material constraints of earthly life. From time to time with a "Please, sir!" he would request that we shoot zebra, impala, and Grant gazelle, exceeding our quota and against all regulations. In explanation he would plead the urgent need of some mountain village in the back of beyond or of some poor devils who had been abandoned deep in the primary forest without food by an unscrupulous employer.

The days went by, and in spite of the efforts of the whole team we had still not been able to capture a *chui,* which, after all, was the main objective of this laborious expedition. We lost count of the number of nights we'd spent in our blinds, and our trackers worked unstintingly, to the point of exhaustion.

This Grant gazelle was taken in Masailand in the Longido hunting area and won an SCI silver medal.

Mrosso remained unperturbed. He rode up front, waving regally to the crowds whenever we passed through a village in a cloud of dust.

One day a typical dawn was breaking over the Engaruka Valley. From the miserable villages, fenced around with thornbush branches to protect the livestock from nocturnal attacks by hyena and lion, a stream of cows, sheep, and goats emerged, lending a misleading air of prosperity to the place.

That morning Mister Mrosso had yet again persuaded us to shoot a Grant gazelle that he needed in order to obtain the good graces of one of the numerous authorities whose favors he curried. We were therefore on the lookout for the next sacrificial victim of our game scout's complex sociopolitical relations when our attention was drawn by the strange behavior of a female ostrich (distinguishable from the male by the more subdued coloring of her plumage). The ostrich is the largest bird on the planet and can weigh more than 300 pounds. It is equipped

113

with legs so powerful it can reach a speed of over 30 MPH and—at least as Masai lore has it—slay a lion with a single kick.

Such was evidently not the intention of this particular bird. The poor thing had trouble walking, stumbling from time to time and dragging its atrophied wings pitifully on the ground. Six and a half feet up, at the end of its long, bare neck, was perched a ridiculous little head with two huge black eyes that rolled in terror at our approach.

The trackers told me I shouldn't be fooled, explaining that it was just a ruse employed by all ratites[1] to ward off predators from their nesting area. And indeed, it wasn't long before our astute helpers spotted in the grass a pile of large eggs that had been laid directly on the ground. I was surprised at how many there were—fifteen altogether. Mrosso told us that each could weigh up to four and a half pounds and that their shells were thick enough to withstand the weight of a man.

Thus informed and without any ill intent, I innocently picked up one of these marvels of nature to take back to camp and present to my wife, who, like wives from time immemorial, was patiently awaiting the return of her hunter.

To my great surprise, Mrosso, who was generally so accommodating, intervened and solemnly reminded me, in his capacity as game scout and protector of the fauna, that "Ostriches are protected animals, and the commerce of their feathers and eggs, etc., has been banned by paragraph 12 of Appendix III of the Washington Convention of 1975." And, moreover, he took a personal interest in these animals, which he considered to be a symbol of the local fauna and were unfortunately endangered by all sorts of illegal trafficking—for which, he gave me to understand, mass tourism was mainly responsible.

Well, really! I was stunned! Red-faced, I quickly put the offending object back. I had to admire the newly found professional conscience exhibited by our protector of the fauna who, nevertheless, generously permitted me to take a few photos. Considering the incident closed, Mister Mrosso took up his place in the front of the truck, signaling that it was time to get back to more pressing matters.

---

[1]Ratites are large, flightless birds with small wings, such as ostriches, rheas, and emus.

The gerenuk (Somali for "giraffe-necked"), an elegant gazelle with a long, slender neck, shares the same territory as the lesser kudu. SCI gold medal. Photograph was taken in the Masai Steppe not far from Mount Kilimanjaro.

The fringe-eared oryx—this one awarded an SCI bronze medal—is the least common of the oryx subspecies. It lives on the Tanzania-Kenya border in the vast semidesert steppes of Amboseli and Tsavo at the foot of Kilimanjaro. The fringe-eared oryx is mistrustful and often aggressive. The Masai say that when attacked, it is capable of killing a lion by stabbing it with its long, daggerlike horns. This oryx was known in Roman times and may be the origin of the unicorn legend.

Feeling somewhat embarrassed, I was about to do likewise when intuition, a sense one develops quickly in Africa, led me to recount the eggs. There were now only fourteen, whereas I was sure I had counted fifteen just minutes before.

Jean-Pierre had been keeping out of this little administrative disagreement, and I approached him discreetly to share my suspicions. Although the whole team was ready to leave and the Toyota already running, he as the organizer of our safari diplomatically asked everyone to step out of the car. In less time than it takes to tell the story, he discovered the fifteenth egg under the very seat occupied by Mister Mrosso. The scout did not miss a beat and claimed, poker-faced, that he had put it there and was planning to offer it to Madam, the hunter's wife.

Do as I say, not as I do!

The safari was taking a worrisome turn. We were threatened with imminent failure, if not ridicule. But this fact did not mitigate in the least the charitable ardor of our game scout, who would stick his head and shoulders out the window, his beret on red, and entreat us with a polite but firm "Please, sir," to stop and help out a school bus that had run out of gasoline or a bush taxi whose suspension had given out. (This last was not at all surprising, given that the five-seat taxi vehicle, whose make was no longer recognizable, was about thirty years old and was carrying some forty passengers—I counted them!) And let's not forget the little Masai shepherds scattered over the immense plain, to whom we were bearing water.

By the fifteenth day of our eighteen-day safari we had killed an amazing quantity of animals: lesser kudu, gerenuk, zebra, gnu, eight or nine Grant gazelle, as many impala, and even an oryx, which had been sacrificed to the elusive god *chui*. Mister Mrosso claimed the lion's share of this mountain of meat, of course, to fulfill his charitable obligations.

And so the fifteenth day dawned. We had slept out in the open. Mister Mrosso lay curled up, his government-issue rifle held tight against his body with the barrel pointing at his eyes. I was the first up. As I contemplated the sun rising on the Rift Valley, I caught an extremely rare glimpse of Mount Kilimanjaro's silhouette in the distance, before it disappeared into the morning mist.

"Very good omen," volunteered Mister Mrosso, who had awakened and joined me with his soft, leporide gait. According to him, the appearance of Kilimanjaro was most definitely a sign of divine good will.

And indeed, as incredible as it may seem to our rational minds, that very night a huge leopard chose to come and devour a haunch of one of the gazelle baits. It cost him his life. Our African comrades were overjoyed.

Mister Mrosso took it upon himself to organize the celebration. He alone had never doubted that we would accomplish our objective. He composed a tune on the spot and hummed it in a quavering voice: "One-Bullet Man shot the big *chui* this night!"

117

ALOYCE S. MROSSO
GAME OFFICE
P.O. BOX 80
MTOWA MBU
ARUSHA TZ.
30.01.2003

Mr. One Bullet Man (Decoster)

How are You? How do you feel? How is your familly? Sure it is a very long time since I saw you in 2001. I think still you remember the name of the camp of Hunting, which is Intercon H. Safaris LTD.

I thank God very much because since that time up to date I'm hokey, and also my familly are hokey.

So Mr. One Bullet how did you enjoy the Chritsmas and the New Year of 2002? May be nothing was bad and you enjoyed well with your familly. If it is so, we have to thank God very much.

As you know, now I'm on leave., until next season which will start on 1st July 2002. Now no hunting. So I do some other jobs. Example patrolling, crop protection, and so on.

Please Sir, really I have a familly problem. I have nothing to do. I'm suffering with school fees. of 4 (four) children. Really is problem and don't know what to do. So please I'm asking for any HELP from You. I have paid have half of the fee's. The other half not yet.

Please Most Greetings To Your Familly. So Until then.

Good bye Mr. ONE........

Without Forgetting

I am Aloyce S. Mrosso.

Sometime after that memorable safari, I received this letter from Mr. Mrosso.

Much to his satisfaction, and mine I must admit, I had in fact been very lucky in always landing my first shot. He saw my marksmanship as a providential tool to be put to good use.

Had the death of the big cat freed us from the strange influence of this African guru?

Well, just as the party was in full swing, Mister Mrosso piped up jocularly, "Please, sir, I would need another zebra."

We quite automatically accepted—and that was when it finally dawned on us that we had become the docile disciples of a pious poacher: Mister Mrosso, the charismatic guide of the Engaruka Valley!

Arusha, Tanzania, October 2002

The Eagle,
the Buffalo, and
the Monitor Lizard

Northern Cameroon

The love of beauty is inseparable from death.

Emil Cioran
The Twilight of the Thoughts

*T*he previous evening, Moussa had been observing a bateleur eagle that was on the ground about to devour a savanna monitor lizard. Moussa surprised us all by running over to the raptor and snatching away its prey.

According to him, only monitors of the savanna variety have all the properties necessary for his purposes. (We will return to this later.) The tracker grabbed the lizard, still alive and twitching, in his long, slender hands and then, using the point of his homemade knife, gutted it to remove a sort of salmon-colored fat with the consistency of semolina. He placed the substance carefully in one of the small amulets he wore across his chest, close to his left breast.

Some buffalo were grazing on a hillside lit by the low-angled rays of the early sun. The lead bull's jet-black coat distinguished him from the cows and the younger bulls. When the bullet hit him, he flipped end over end and thudded to the bottom of the steep slope. Then, as the rest of the frightened herd made off at a full gallop into the bush, he got up and slipped into some long, dry grass that had been spared by the fires.

The small buffalo[1] was now alone. A little blood was dripping from the wound on his chest, spreading a red stain over the bronze reflections of his coat.

---

[1]Cameroon is home to a species of dwarf buffalo *(Nanus savanus)* that are brave and aggressive in spite of their small size.

"The old buffalo rolled like a rock into the bed of the mayo."

"As they walked, our three trackers had fashioned torches out of long braids of dry grass, using

them to set fire to the large swaths of dry scrub through which the trail led us."

On the light morning breeze he picked up the scent of humans, a smell that all wild animals dread. He knew instinctively that he was engaged in a fight for his life. Did he also know that as the hours passed, the precious blood that seeped from his wounded dewlap would become a deadly Ariadne's thread that would inevitably lead his merciless stalkers to him?

Moussa stopped at the brink of a deep *bako*. With a practiced gesture, he took the amulet of yellowish leather that held the monitor's fat he had confiscated from the eagle the day before. He then set about gathering branches, selecting them with care. Next, he cut some straw with his machete and lit a fire with it into which he threw the sacred wood, adding a pinch of the magic substance as well as a few other mysterious ingredients extracted from his various amulets. Later he revealed to us that his precious packets contained porcupine quills, hyena excrement, aardvark teeth, pangolin scales, and verses from the Koran.

When he judged the moment right, he stood where he would be engulfed in the smoke swirling up from the fire. Then, confident of the invulnerability his charms conferred on him, he marched back to the head of our little troop and plunged fearlessly into the forest where the wounded buffalo had disappeared.

We whites advanced cautiously, mindful that another hunter had recently been killed in similar circumstances. I gripped my gun hard and held it at the ready, even though it was beginning to cut into the palm of my hand.

We followed the animal's trail for hours. As they walked, our three trackers had fashioned torches out of long braids of dry grass. These they used to set fire to the large swaths of dry scrub through which the trail led us, starting huge blazes that were powerfully fanned by the hot, dry wind from the east.

Guided by instinct no doubt, the black bull was now making for the top of a mountain, Hossere Boumba, realizing that there was nowhere to hide in the savanna lower down. In his climb to the top of the mountain he led us along narrow paths, and as we followed him we came across forgotten sites, traces of terraced villages strewn with broken pottery, apparently abandoned for many years. Haman, a tracker, later explained that these were the remains of the homes of his Duru ancestors, who had once fled to the back country to escape the slave traffickers from the north.

The sun was at its zenith. We were very hot and thirsty, prey to tsetse flies and the painful stinging plants that grew among the dense vegetation. The bull's wound had closed. A little bloody mucus oozed from its swollen muzzle.

Some reddish froth in the mud near a watering hole told us that the fugitive had rested there for a moment. He had drunk a great deal of the brackish water and it was weighing him down; he was losing ground. The way his back was hunched indicated that toxins had entered his bloodstream and were poisoning him; his muscles were gradually stiffening.

We continued on our way through a magnificent landscape. As far as the eye could see, right to the banks of the Faro River, a breathtaking panorama was spread out before us: the Koti Manga plateau, a monumental mosaic in shades of green, ochre, gray; a damask of patches of laterite; forests of Daniellia; and fan palms with curious orangy-yellow fruits. In the distance plumes of smoke still rose from the fires we had lit to protect ourselves from ambush by the animal we had been tracking without respite for seven or eight hours now.

Moussa was spurred on by an unshakable belief in his own infallibility. He was sure that our goal now lay within reach. Not wishing to be overtaken by darkness, he hastened his pace, forcing us along. It was hard going.

On the mountainside, streams rose and trickled thinly down through shallow hollows like gashes on a giant's face. Perhaps it was in one of these remote havens that the animal had been born some ten years before and, as a calf at his dam's side, experienced the first challenges of a harsh, perilous existence.

Suddenly, Moussa stopped short and sniffed the air, like a cat. Perched on a large slab of basalt, we all peered down attentively at the foliage of the *bako* we were about to enter. As a precautionary measure, the tracker signaled to us to climb a bit higher up the steep wall.

He put a finger to his lips and murmured, "*Mbogo.*"

Amidst a crashing of breaking branches and falling stones, a dark mass erupted out of the foliage as the buffalo attempted a last pathetic charge with what little energy he had left. A shot thundered through the hills. A pinkish veil dropped over the old buffalo's eyes, and he tottered and rolled like a rock into the bed of the *mayo* that might once have been his birthplace.

An eagle with speckled, ash-colored wings took flight from a nearby ledge, its screech a strident war cry that rent the evening air as the bird flew off. As if bearing away the animal's last breath, the eagle gradually faded into the vast African sky.

Koti Manga Camp, northern Cameroon, February 2003

The Price of Things

Northern Cameroon

Woman is a delicious fruit with a tough skin.
Only the toothless break their teeth on it.

Cameroonian Proverb

That year, 2004, two of our usual group did not make it to our annual hunt. Our friend Pierre-Alain, a.k.a. the Colonel, and Sali, the cook, had gone to join their ancestors in the hereafter. The wheel of time was turning—for whites and blacks alike. Michel seemed to drag his left leg a bit more, and I was having trouble buckling my belt at the usual notch.

The eland, however, were as elusive as ever and led us on interminable marathons for seven, eight, sometimes even ten hours at a stretch. We were all worn out.

But then, on the eleventh day, we managed to cut them off and shoot the lead bull, which now lay dead on the dusty ground of the Koti Manga plateau. Michel was stretched out in the shade of a stately Senegal mahogany tree, his head resting on an old sack. The men were already busy butchering the antelope. As I watched the scene, I couldn't help but sense a hint of "last safari" in the air around our aging group[1]. When the work was done we started back, the trackers heavily laden with fresh meat.

---

[1]My somber premonition unfortunately turned out to be correct, at least for Michel. This was to be his last safari. Struck down by illness, he was not able to accompany me the following year, and I continued my journeying alone. But without him, it would never be the same again. He is one of those exceptional people who bring an added dimension and a spark of magic to an otherwise ordinary adventure.

"The eland lay dead on the dusty ground of the Koti Manga plateau."

As we approached the encampment, the men burst enthusiastically into the victory chant they saved for special occasions. And for these old hands, the death of the *yamoussa* was certainly such an occasion.

Yamoussa Allah M Barima A Watina
Yamoussa Allah M Barima A Dillina
Yamoussa Allah M Barima A Hottina
Yamoussa M Barima Papa Eddy.

Eland, God has killed you, you are dead
Eland, God has killed you, you are gone
Eland, God has killed you, you are gone to heaven
Eland, who killed you?
Papa Eddy.

Michel, more soberly, remarked that this was the tenth giant eland we had shot together. That evening, as was the custom, we gathered everyone around the fire with beer, Coca-Cola, and whiskey to celebrate our hard-won victory. The Africans smoked strange cigarettes that they rolled from small rectangles of paper cut out of the school notebooks of the young villagers who had exchanged them for a bit of dried beef. In some places you could make out the writing on the paper.

I stood back and smiled as I watched Moussa, who had never set foot in a schoolroom, negligently transforming La Fontaine's fables or Archimedes' theorem into wreaths of smoke that rose into the starry night, perhaps taking with them a little of the soul of our poets to distant galaxies that the Sara tribesman had never heard of. At that moment, his innocence made him master of the universe, and secretly I envied him.

Michel knew the Africans well, and conversed with them easily.

"Issa, what religion?" he asked one of them out of the blue.

"Protestant Christian, Papa K," replied Issa, emphasizing the "Protestant."

"How many wives?"

"One only!" replied the tall Duru tribesman with a genuine look of reproach.

"What about you, Moussa? You're Muslim, aren't you? How many wives?"

"Two and a half, boss," the Sara mumbled, somewhat bitterly.

"Two and a half? What do you mean?" asked my old friend. "Are you sharing a woman with another man?"

"No, no!" protested the tracker. "I say two and a half because I not finish paying for third wife."

"Hum . . . Well, now, let's see," Michel went on. "What do you have to pay the parents for this new wife?"

"Hundred and fifty thousand francs[2]. But there are many other suitors," Moussa said, visibly peeved. "I must also bring chest with linen cloth for the mother and slippers for the father. It is much money!"

"How old is she, this young beauty of yours?" Michel asked, apparently sympathetic to the young man's plight.

"I not know exactly," said the man. He gave it a little thought and added, "Maybe thirteen, no more."

"And what about you, Haman?"

The head tracker pretended he hadn't heard, but Michel insisted, teasing him gently.

"A Duru woman, Haman. What must you offer the family for a Duru woman?"

"Three hundred thousand francs, if she is virgin," Haman finally acknowledged. He had come to know us and was wary of our hypocritical questions.

"Three hundred thousand! Double the price of a Sara woman! Why such a difference?"

"It is because the Duru woman," Haman explained, "she work hard in the house and in the field, even when she has the child. She has much courage— much courage!"

Seizing the moment to enter into this all-important debate, I inquired mischievously, "And a Fulbe woman, what would she be worth?"

"Fifty thousand francs," said Issa without any hesitation, mockingly, with a big grin that revealed his filed-down teeth.

"Fifty thousand francs!" I repeated, pretending to be shocked. "Fifty thousand

---

[2]At that time, 100,000 CFA francs (currency of the African Financial Community) was the equivalent of about U.S. $180.

francs for a Fulbe woman, the most beautiful of all the creatures in Africa!"

"It is true," he replied in a rueful tone, "it is true. The Fulbe woman is very pretty, very pretty, but she work very little, very little. And," he mumbled, a little embarrassed, "if you leave hut for too long, she go quickly to other man."

It sounded as if some old bitterness was resurfacing here. I was about to put an end to the conversation, but could not help asking, somewhat disingenuously, "And one of the Bororo's steers, what would that be worth?"

"Four hundred thousand francs, Papa D," shot back Moussa, adding with relish, "and even more if he's a very big one with long black and white horns."

Koti Manga, Cameroon, January 2004

Return to Yabassi

Equatorial Forest Region of Southern Cameroon

For history is made with tools, not with ideas; and everything is changed by economic conditions—art, philosophy, love, virtue—truth itself!

Joseph Conrad
The Secret Agent

The safari was over and we had to make a stop in Douala, southern Cameroon, to wait for a flight to Paris. I had suspected for quite some time that Michel, though he would never admit it, would have loved to return to the scene of his first stay in Africa. Years back he had been sent to Yabassi by an uncompromising school board with whom he did not see eye to eye and had been appointed to teach there, in the most inhospitable area of the equatorial forest of southern Cameroon. This town was not far, by the way, from the rubber plantations where the French writer Louis-Ferdinand Céline, at odds with society, had himself lived in self-imposed exile forty years earlier. My friend and the author of *Journey to the End of the Night* had many other points in common, but that would be another story altogether.

The fortunes of life sometimes work in our favor. By chance, one of the employees of the seedy Douala hotel we had chosen in an attempt to save money came from Yabassi.

Monkey hunter in the equatorial forest.

Early one morning, with his help and without Michel's knowledge, I managed with some difficulty to persuade a taxi driver—who was either more enterprising or needier than his colleagues—to drive us to Yabassi, which was about sixty miles from Douala in the depths of the equatorial forest.

It was most unfortunate that our driver, a Bamileke tribesman, chose to take a shortcut through the notoriously dangerous Bassa quarter, one of the worst in Douala, which is hardly one of central Africa's most welcoming cities to begin with. It is almost impossible to accurately describe the atmosphere of the place. The decaying facades of the colonial-era buildings, vestiges of France's presence here, had no doors or windows anymore. They stood surrounded by a multitude of shacks built of planks, bricks, plastic, and metal sheeting, piled together without any attempt at harmony. The disparate population huddled on either side of a potholed avenue that looked as though it had just been bombed.

This apocalyptic decor housed a swarming mass of people of all ages who spent their days wandering about aimlessly. Some were flamboyantly dressed in clothing that advertised the world's most prestigious brands; others wore tattered shirts that hung from their shoulders by the seams. Most went barefoot or wore rubber sandals cut from the tires of the wrecked cars that lay rusting by the roadside.

The driver was very tense as he tried to force his way through the throng that threatened to engulf our vehicle. He did his best to avoid the huge, craterlike potholes in which children paddled together with ducks and pigs. Now and again, young men, their eyes reddened by the abuse of kola, shouted an angry, hate-filled stream of abuse at us. Their invective was accompanied with explicit, obscene gestures, to the dismay of our driver, who was as worried for himself as for his taxi, which was in pretty bad shape as it was.

The few policemen we encountered in this huge ghetto that sprawled on for miles, far from ensuring our safety, were only interested in fleecing us on some pretext or other. Thankfully, we finally made it through to the other side of that hellhole and entered the imposing equatorial forest.

As we drove along, teeming humanity gave way to virgin mangrove, the insults of hoodlums to the rhythmic singing of tropical birds, the stench of the slum to the fragrance of luxuriant vegetation. The few dwellings that lined the trail on which we now traveled seemed deserted, but although we saw not a single soul, we felt that we were being watched from deep within the forest. It was strangely disquieting.

Gradually, we entered the territory of a strange and mysterious fauna: rare yellow-backed duiker, bongo (magnificent antelope with white-striped chestnut coats), and innumerable colorful varieties of monkeys that peered at us from high up in the tall trees.

The trip was long and arduous. Several times we had to browbeat the taxi driver to dissuade him from turning back. After a few hours' drive, during which we met no one except a few monkey hunters, we finally made it to the banks of the Wouri River, on the other side of which lay the capital of Bassa country.

A surprise awaited us at the entrance to the town of Yabassi. Emerging in all their majesty from an ocean of greenery, larger than life, in white ceramic with sky-blue ornament, stood the most amazing Virgin Mother and Child I had ever seen! The artist who had created the Madonna statue had manifestly shrugged off his Bantu culture and ingenuously given her the delicate features and inscrutable expression of an oriental woman. The pedestal on which she stood bore a plaque indicating that we were in the presence of Our Lady of Prompt Succor.

The winds of history had blown over Yabassi for almost fifty years, and the few buildings that remained from the colonial era had seen better days. The prison, the hospital, the prefecture, and a few shutdown hotels bore witness to a glorious past, while all around a proliferation of tumbledown houses of mud or wood had been built on the remains of the old concessions.

The school itself was still standing, and in relatively good shape. On this last Saturday in January it was completely empty. But Michel was shocked as he entered what had once been his quarters, next door. Although the exterior of the building, constructed in brick before 1914 by the Germans, had withstood the onslaught of time, the inside had been vandalized by the villagers. Anything that could be carried off had been pillaged: windows, doors, flooring, toilets, washbasins. Nothing that could be dismantled had been left.

As we contemplated the damage, a pleasant young man came over to us. He was the schoolteacher. You can imagine his surprise when he learned that the elder of the two white men who had wandered into the building was his predecessor of almost a half-century before—he himself was barely twenty-five years old. To this young man we might just as well have been Martians who had

The icon of Yabassi: Our Lady of Prompt Succor.

dropped out of the sky. But the old and the new teacher soon hit it off. I was pleased to hear Michel, usually so reserved, telling the young teacher how he had decided back in 1957 to build such and such a building, plant the large mango trees that shaded the courtyard, and have the mahogany desks made at which generations of little schoolchildren had toiled for so many years. And in the course of their conversation, I was amused to hear Michel berate his successor for the bad condition of the roofs, the worrisome state of this or that termite-ridden beam, or for not having replaced the broken door and window frames.

When we had finished inspecting the school, our new friend offered to take us to the only restaurant still in business, all the others having folded long before for lack of clients. The Gueto was located on the central square, which had been renamed Place de l'Indépendance. In this dilapidated building, somewhat protected from the sun by a wooden veranda, the lady in charge lay fast asleep on a mat on the floor.

The schoolteacher gently prodded her awake with his toe, and as she unfolded her long legs and rose languidly to her feet, I noticed how beautiful she was. Surprised to find white customers in her establishment, she indicated three cast-iron pots that were set on stools and contained the day's menu. We had a choice of bush-meat stew marinating in a greenish sauce out of which peeked the tail of a giant rat and the hand of a cercopithecus monkey; a bouillabaisse of catfish in an inky sauce; and a vegetable hotpot in which I could identify cassava, yams, and plantain. The driver greedily threw himself on the meat while we unenthusiastically fell back on the fish.

Delighted to have company, the young lady readily answered all my friend's questions. Michel very soon realized that none of his old acquaintances was still alive. It is true that in Africa, fifty years is an eternity. She also told us that the last whites to have spent any time in Yabassi had been a family of Korean or perhaps Chinese foresters five or six years before, and I realized where the sculptor of the Madonna, which dated back to about that time, had gotten his inspiration.

Our hostess dreamed of visiting France, and especially wanted to see and touch snow. She was prepared to do anything to get there and even proposed marriage to me, which, according to her, was the only way she was sure to get a visa for Europe. Wanting to please us, she turned up the volume on the radio. The music program was suddenly interrupted, ironically, by a commentator

Michel and the teacher: The past and the present come together.

announcing in excellent French that President Paul Biya was in Geneva, along with most of the members of his administration, where they were "firmly establishing Cameroon's place on the international scene."

Michel pointed out that with less than half of the budget allocated for this impressive diplomatic delegation, they could have repaired all the public buildings and other communal infrastructures of Yabassi and the surrounding region.

We were just finishing our gourmet meal when a strange parade suddenly appeared. Waving banners depicting the presidential couple, a burlesque procession of fat, perspiring matrons in European dress waddled along beside their VIP husbands, undertaking several tours of the square as a sign of support for their "dear" president. This all took place under the indifferent gaze of young Bassas who sat astride their old motorbikes, unmoved by this sycophantic display of allegiance to authorities who had probably never even set foot in Yabassi.

It was getting late and our driver, who had finally finished gorging himself, was determined to leave before dark, especially because he wanted to take another route, safer but much longer, to avoid the Bassa quarter. I took leave of my would-be fiancée, who was very disappointed not to be coming along. Michel shook hands with the schoolteacher, who was clearly delighted by this unexpected encounter, though I am not sure he fully understood the significance of the gesture, which symbolized, to my mind, fifty years of history.

As we once again crossed the Wouri, Michel reminisced about the time long ago when, as a young school inspector, he rode down the river in the long pirogues that the Bodiman boatmen had hewn out of the trunks of huge trees from the equatorial forest, the same forest that engulfed us as we left Yabassi behind, probably forever.

Douala, Cameroon, January 2004

Diamond Eyes

Northern Cameroon

To my wife, Maria Dolores.

The bush at dawn is the world on the first morning of creation. The animals roam tranquilly, as if in a landscape by Jan "Velvet" Brueghel. It is a charmed moment; the gods seem to have calmed down and, for the time being, have stopped persecuting earth's creatures.

The lion has stopped roaring. The mosquitoes and tsetse flies have vanished. The antelope graze serenely, and the air is mild and soothing. White or black, rich or poor, young or old and weary, the traveler is filled with hope for the new day. Even the sun that will soon blast this paradise with its scorching heat has let up for a few hours.

We walked in silence, still wrapped up in our woolen jackets. At my side, Maria Dolores (Lola), a Spanish madonna, was more beautiful than ever and reminded me of Audrey Hepburn in *Sabrina*.

We made our way along the roof of Africa, our gaze lost in the glorious dawn landscape that went on and on into infinity. But of course it was only a truce, a fleeting rebirth. The wind too had abated. It flowed gently from east to west, blowing steadily as if to spare us the sudden changes of direction it generally makes during the hot hours of the day, making it impossible to approach the big game.

The professional hunter who accompanied us hadn't bothered to bring his rifle with him, and if mine was slung across Moussa's shoulder, it was only because the Sara tribesman, an experienced tracker, had decided out of habit or professional conscience to bring it along.

We found ourselves on a laterite plateau with little plant life. The sun's horizontal rays cast a golden light on the dry grasses and the shrubs, whose long shadows stretched and blended into the brick-colored earth.

The lead man stopped, extended a long, sinewy arm toward the bush, and softly murmured, as though hesitant to break the silence of this endless highland, "*Koba!*" *Koba* is the generic name given in West Africa to the roan antelope (Hippotragus equinus), once found in great abundance from the Sahel to the Tropic of Capricorn.

This antelope, with its scimitar-shaped horns that curl back toward the neck, is the size of a race horse and has the same incomparable way of galloping nostrils to the wind. It frequents rocky regions with scant vegetation where the wild gardenias, its favorite food, grow.

I had already shot a good dozen roan antelope in Senegal, in the Central African Republic, and in Cameroon, and so there was no reason I should be particularly interested in this one. But the devil that sat on my shoulder goaded me on.

The tracker was insistent: "Very good," he said, with just the right amount of emphasis. Moussa, however, was crafty. We had traveled the bush together for so long that he knew me well. He knew how to arouse my interest subtly, without appearing too eager, which, as he was well aware, would have instantly produced the opposite reaction and earned him a curt remark such as, "You Africans, don't you ever get enough? You won't be happy until you've exterminated every last animal in the region!"

"Very long," Moussa added with hypocritical indifference, referring to the length of the horns, which was not in the least important to him. There is not an African on the continent who gives a fig for a trophy; the only thing that interests them is the meat—above all, the meat of the *koba*.

I felt the members of my little team turn to look at me, one by one, including my lovely Andalusian wife. In moments such as these, even the most seasoned adventurer, one who has explored Africa's every nook and cranny and sworn up and down he'll never be taken in again . . . gets taken in again. When the hopes of the whole "tribe" are pinned on you and you hold the divine power to decide the fate of a coveted prey, the predatory instinct that we all have deep inside us

A roan antelope (Hippotragus equinus) *with white face markings.*

nearly always wins out. And so I made my first concession, my first mistake, and raised my binocular.

The *koba* was indeed there, alone, moving slowly and carefully picking over the fragrant, gardenia-scented provender, bathed in the sun's warm halo of light. This was an old male, his thick horns fairly long, but not as long as that scoundrel Moussa would have had me believe. The cunning tracker was already holding out my rifle to me with the artless gesture of he who knows what needs to be done, as though it was understood between us insiders. Unconsciously, almost as a precaution, just in case . . . I took it. My second mistake!

Lola and the others were watching me wordlessly, with the falsely contrite air of the righteous as the death sentence is read out. What I didn't know was that the evil spirit hovering over my shoulder had chosen me as the first victim of its nefarious pranks.

Unhurriedly, I aimed and squeezed off a shot. To my surprise and mortification, I missed the target, which was standing only about a hundred yards from us. At the sound of the shot, the old antelope gave a start, trotted off a few yards, and continued his meal as though nothing had happened.

My pride was wounded, and though I should have spared the animal and let him go free, I aimed again more carefully and took another shot at the big *koba*, hitting him in the shoulder. He slumped to the ground, then immediately got up again and came toward us at a full gallop.

Since we happened to be standing in the path of the unfortunate animal, at first I thought it was just coincidence. When he was within forty yards of us, I hit him with a second shot in the same place. This caused him to stumble again, but he continued his angry charge. It was then clear that he meant to gore us.

Finally, hit for the third time full in the chest, the brave antelope fell in a cloud of dust, his horns tearing up the earth, less than ten yards from where we stood . . . petrified. The wonderful morning had almost ended in disaster, with the evil spirit very nearly getting the upper hand.

Quite recovered from my fright, I approached the beautiful antelope where he lay stone-dead, his ringed horns driven into the red earth. The eyes, though lifeless, seemed to be observing me from behind the painted mask, the pupils glowing like embers.

The eyes are said to be the mirror of the soul. I had already observed this strange phenomenon in the bravest animals, which, even in death, continue to stare at you, almost accusingly.

As I turned away I met my wife's loving gaze. Silvery reflections sparkled in her smiling eyes, their pupils shining like diamonds. I was heartened, and the sadness that had begun to creep into my soul lifted.

Koti Manga Camp, northern Cameroon, 2006

Hatari!

Northern Cameroon

*To all the professional hunters who risk losing their lives,
and sometimes their souls, to their dangerous vocation.*

f there is one topic of conversation that crops up time and again and is
guaranteed to spark animated argument among even the most phlegmatic
hunters, it has to be the debate over which is the most dangerous of the African
big-game animals. Opinions naturally differ, based as they are on personal
experience. Most hunters have witnessed accidents, or themselves been involved
in one, sometimes with dire consequences.

In the course of my own hunting career I have been attacked with varying
degrees of ferocity by lion, elephant, buffalo, hippo, and even, as described in the
last chapter, by a roan. The professional hunters encountered in hunting camps
over the past forty years have regaled me with countless stories, many of them quite
harrowing. There is not an adventurer among them who does not bear the scars
of a confrontation with a lion, a leopard or, more often, a buffalo. I myself came
within a hair's breadth of being killed in an attempt to stop a charging lion that had
been wounded by one of my companions on the banks of the Youhamba River in
northern Central African Republic. (See chapter entitled "The Accident.")

We will leave aside the rhino, which unfortunately is hunted nowadays only
in the enclosed preserves of South Africa. (The reader will know by now that
this is not at all my kind of hunting.) And for the sake of argument, let us also
leave aside the crocodile, whose nefarious activities are confined to wetlands and

---

*Hatari means danger in Swahili.

are more of a threat to the local populations that have the misfortune to share its natural habitat.

I should remind the reader that some apparently harmless animals can actually inflict terrible injuries on the unwary. In this category, for example, you can include the Hippotraginae, such as the roan, sable, and oryx, and even some Tragelaphinae: bongo, sitatunga, and bushbuck. That list should also contain the ostrich, which the Masai say can break a lion's neck with one swipe of a paw.

I am going to limit my considerations here to the five big-game animals that are generally considered the most aggressive. Although statistically it rates first place, I would rank the hippo last. Indeed, it is well known that this brutal pachyderm is responsible for more fatal accidents than any other animal on the African continent. I do not question that fact, but its main victims are either hapless fishermen attacked in their boats or the unfortunate women and children who spend their lives on the banks of the rivers and lakes throughout sub-Saharan Africa, where numerous pods of hippo still flourish. This bad-tempered, ungainly, three-ton bulldozer is likely to attack without the slightest provocation, its wrath aroused by the mere fact of finding someone in its path. The hippo's speed and agility are surprising: It can run at over twenty miles per hour, leaving its generally unarmed victims little chance of escape.

Hunters, on the other hand, are less-easy prey. The hippo is not a discreet animal, and the hunter can take it at the water's edge or even in the water. When wounded, it dives down deep and comes up only for air. Hunting hippo entails no dangerous pursuits through tall grass and thickets, so an experienced, patient hunter will not be taken unaware. The beast can be easily dispatched with one well-aimed bullet to the brain.

The African elephant, until the mid-twentieth century, was generally considered a tolerant, easy-going animal that accepted the intrusion of humans into its vast territories. However, over time the elephant—persecuted by ivory traffickers, massacred by veritable armies of mercenaries on the payroll of young states freed of the restrictions imposed by colonial administration, and plagued by ruthless poachers with assault weapons—has gradually and radically changed its habits in order to survive. No longer the loud extrovert it used to be, it has become secretive, paranoid, and unpredictable. It is constantly on the move, and its formerly gentle nature has been replaced by an aggressive behavior dictated by mistrust and by

Charging elephant in Tsavo National Park, Kenya, 1972.

its intelligence. As far as I know, this is a unique phenomenon among the larger mammals. Today elephant can be extremely menacing, especially the cows. To protect their calves, they are wont to charge at any moment for no apparent reason, making them the most dangerous of *un*wounded animals.

And yet, hunting accidents are relatively rare. An elephant is hard to miss, and it does give warning. Usually a loud trumpeting or an intimidating charge will do the trick and put everyone in their place.

And what about the lion, you may be wondering. Albeit with some hesitation, and despite an altercation I once had with one, I would award only third place in our ranking to this animal—on which we have conferred, perhaps too hastily, the august title of "king of all the animals." This majestic feline is considered the most fearsome in the teeming inventory of Africa's animals, but in my humble opinion it does not always live up to its reputation.

Contrary to legend and popular belief, this famous "man-eater" often seems lazy, nonchalant, even timid. Given a preference, it will go for easy prey such as rodents, monkeys, and warthogs, eschewing buffalo and sharp-horned antelope. It will avoid attempting a risky attack, preferring to hunt in a group rather than on its own. Only when driven by starvation will it take any chances.

The first reflex of a wounded lion is to flee. The lion is extremely vulnerable to bullet wounds and will usually be found dead or dying not far from where it was shot. Because a lion almost always precedes its attack with a warning roar, an experienced hunter is rarely taken by surprise and can fell the four-hundred-pound cat with a single shot to the chest. Only when exhausted, cornered, and desperate to save its hide does a lion turn mean. At lightning speed it will cover the distance separating the two of you in a few bounds to go for your throat. Can you blame it?

The second spot on the podium should go to the leopard—though again this is only my personal view. The leopard, unlike the lion, is a loner. It prowls at night, and its path seldom crosses that of hunters. Even though it is reputed to devour the little children who guard the goats on the Masai Steppe, it rarely attacks humans. I must admit, though, that I myself have never had to do battle with this superb feline, as the five leopard I have shot all died on the spot. This success is, however, no great feat, given that the leopard is generally hunted at dusk, from a blind, with the aid of bait strung up on the branch of a tree near which tracks have been spotted. The leopard is usually shot at close range while it is busy tearing at

Leopard shot in the Selous Game Reserve, Tanzania, September 2000.

After the battle: The small West African buffalo weighs in at little more than nine hundred pounds but is nonetheless an extremely aggressive animal. Unlike its cousins, the Cape buffalo and the central African aequinoctialis, its horns do not have a central boss joining them in the middle. Its coat can vary from a light reddish color to a blackish brown.

the meat so generously put out for it. Even a very large male seldom weighs more than 180 pounds, and, as with other felines, bullet wounds are generally fatal.

But beware! A leopard that does survive a bullet is not going to flee to safety, as would a lion. It will almost always lie in wait for its attackers, perfectly camouflaged in the grass thanks to its spotted coat and its ability to blend into the ground cover. As night falls, the hunt becomes more difficult. The hunters—wearing headlamps to light the way and often clad in thick leather jackets, aware that at any moment the cat may charge out at them as soon as they unwittingly come within reach—know that any mistake may be their last.

The leopard is the most courageous and the most ferocious of all the cats. It waits till the very last second to pounce on its pursuer and tear him to shreds, ripping frenziedly at the upper body with all four limbs at once. And it is a doomed hunter who misses his shot—that leopard will show him no mercy.

But for all that, and in spite of the leopard's chilling determination, the title of most fearsome animal of the African bush belongs to the buffalo, in all its many varieties—be they the big *caffers* of the Cape, the aequinoctialis of central Africa, or the little western buffalo. To my eyes all buffalo represent the hunter's greatest danger. Some of them seem indestructible and, even riddled with bullets, appear immune to pain. When wounded they feign flight, the better to lure you onto their terrain of choice (the tall grasses and the *bakos*), where they wait for you with every intention of making mincemeat of you.

We all know of seasoned hunters and experienced guides who have been seriously mutilated or killed by buffalo, and not because they made any mistakes. They lost their battles purely by being outsmarted.

Lion will flee and put up a fight only when cornered. Elephant will threaten, give you fair warning, before charging. But the perfidious buffalo will lie in ambush, lurking in the high grasses or hidden deep in some dark *bako*, intent on tearing your guts out, no matter how much pain it may be suffering. Buffalo never surrender, and that is what sets them apart from the other big game; as long as there is still breath in them, they will not give up.

Like all hunters who have shot buffalo, I have had to stop the angry charge of a wounded bull on several occasions, luckily without mishap. And yet, one story very nearly did not have a happy ending.

I was hard on the heels of a herd of Lord Derby eland with Jean-Jacques Dumont, an experienced hunter possessed of a most amazing sangfroid. This was several years ago in northern Cameroon, at the heart of a vast territory that stretches from the banks of the Faro River to the foothills of the Hossere Boumba range. We were crossing a volcanic crater where we often hunted, drawn by the beauty of the place and the abundant game. There we would generally come across a few roan, a herd of hartebeest, or a bushbuck.

That morning at around ten o'clock, as the sun was warming things up, two buffalo were grazing right in the center of a steep-walled basin only two hundred yards from us. I had no intention of disturbing them, being interested only in eland. Jean-Jacques, though, after quickly observing them through his binocular, which I had not even bothered to do, said, "It's an old bull with a young page." After a moment's silence, he added, "He's fabulous—take him!"

I was not keen on this idea, and by then the animals had either spotted us or caught wind of us and were galloping off. "Shoot!" the PH insisted. "That's a record trophy for these parts!"

Seeing that they would soon be out of reach, I squeezed off a hasty shot without taking careful aim, something one simply does not do.

"You got him!"

The darker of the two, the old bull, had staggered before disappearing into some bush. I was sure he had been hit, but not happy about it. One does not shoot a buffalo on impulse, especially at that distance, record trophy or not. I shouldn't have heeded my friend.

The trackers rapidly found the blood trail. The stains were few, dullish red, and quite high up on the foliage—a bad sign. The bullet had probably hit the paunch, the worst place. A shot like that means nothing but trouble. First of all, it is never decisive and condemns the animal to a slow and agonizing death, and infection will set in early on, making the poor animal dangerously aggressive. Furthermore, wounds to the paunch or the guts bleed very little, making it extremely difficult to track down the animal. I had acted like a rank amateur.

We set off in pursuit with Gadal and Moussa, the trackers, taking the lead. Right behind them and in front of me was Jean-Jacques with his .458 Winchester Magnum at the ready. The two bearers and my wife, Maria Dolores, walked behind me single-file.

Allow me to digress here for a moment: The reader may have noticed that I have barely mentioned weapons and ammunition in these stories. In Africa the important thing, to my mind, is to possess a solid, dependable, easy-to-handle rifle with a good-quality, well-zeroed scope. The difficulties lie not so much in the shot itself as in the conditions.

Faced with a buffalo, a lion, or an elephant, the hunter must remain cool, in control of his emotions. Good knowledge of the animal is essential, enabling him to distinguish at a glance a beautiful trophy in the midst of several dozen head and seize the occasion. So often, a few seconds are all one has to aim a shot into the hollow under the shoulder of an old eland partially masked by his protective females and blurred by vegetation. The situation makes the greater difference—not how sophisticated your gun is or the type of ammunition you use. If you have a good .375 H&H with a well-zeroed, light-sensitive scope, you can confidently take any big-game animal on the African continent without putting your party in danger. Your rifle will do what you need it to do if you know how to become one with it, make it a natural extension of your arm, can line up the cross hairs of your scope with your target, and possess the reflexes to react promptly but without undue haste.

Back to the hunt: I looked at my watch. Already noon. No longer could we find any sign of blood, but the trackers were still on the spoor of the two buffalo, which were still traveling together. Predictably, they were headed straight for the mountains. We moved along in silence. I was uneasy, worried about my wife.

We were following the course of Mayo Dogba, one of the main tributaries of the Faro River, which flows into the Bénoué, a magnificent river that snakes along until it joins up with the great Niger before spilling into the Gulf of Guinea.

Suddenly, Moussa extended a long, sinewy arm to indicate a dark mass that I would not have made out had it not been for the flick of a tail chasing away the flies. There they were. The two buffalo did not move; they were nearly invisible in the dark shade. We could pick out only their hindquarters. Jean-Jacques motioned to me to move closer. But our move alerted the buffalo, which took off amid a great crashing of branches.

I knew that as time wore on, the old bull would eventually make the connection between the unbearable pain that was wracking his body and the men who had been tracking him for hours.

I sent Maria Dolores a look of encouragement. She was keeping up with us well and I appreciated her stamina, but I had a sense of foreboding. Gadal slowed his pace, retraced his steps, and set off again in a wide curve, almost a perfect circle, examining the ground. He came back to us with the news that the buffalo had separated. This was not good. It meant that the wounded animal was exhausted and had neither the energy nor the will to try to escape us. Sooner or later he was going to confront us, or lay us a trap.

We stayed with the *mayo*, walking either along its bed or up on the banks eight or nine feet above the riverbed, which had been deeply etched by runoff from the torrential monsoon rains that batter the flanks of the mountain year in, year out.

The old bull knew instinctively what he had to do to get rid of us. He about-faced and returned in our direction on a path parallel to his outgoing one, and then took up a position in some brush deep in the *bako*. Minutes later he caught our scent, let us pass, and then shot out like a cannonball behind us just as we—and I can only thank our lucky stars—had climbed up onto the bank where the sparse vegetation would make our progress easier. He summoned all his energy to struggle up the wall of earth between us; fortunately for us, it was very steep. Without pause, Jean-Jacques fired off two shots with his .458 at point-blank range, and I fired two from my .375 H&H. The animal fell into the water, got up again, and fled back into the bushes.

The bearers had dropped whatever they were carrying and taken refuge among the branches. I looked around and was relieved to see that one of them had led my wife to safety behind a large tree.

Gadal and Moussa escorted us as we moved carefully along the riverbank, fingers on our triggers, toward the bushes where the buffalo was hiding, thinking we would find him dead or dying (after all, he'd taken four bullets at near point-blank range!). There was not a sound—not the slightest sign of life. And then, just as I was about to drop my guard, sure that the beast was done for, he popped up like a jack-in-the-box and charged again as powerfully as before, in another valiant attempt to scramble to the top of the bank where we stood waiting, guns at the ready. Four more shots rang out. The bull rolled into the stream, got up yet again, climbed up the opposite side, and then lay down out in the open on bare ground.

"The bull pulled himself up onto his legs again with lightning speed, turned about, and charged us for a third time."

At this juncture, a deep trench separated us from the buffalo, which was lying about thirty yards away with his back toward us. I did a quick count of the shots we had fired, all of which had definitely hit their target: five from the .375, including the first one that morning, and four from the .458. Surely the bull's best option now would have been to gather what strength he had left and flee as far as possible from the men with their guns who had inflicted such terrible wounds on him. It's certainly what any other wild animal would have done.

Jean-Jacques asked me whether he should put the dying bull out of its misery with a shot to the spine. I agreed: His rifle was more powerful than mine. My friend took careful aim and fired off the tenth shot. It went through the bull's back—missing the backbone. And then, incredibly, the bull pulled himself up onto his legs again with lightning speed, turned about, and charged us for the third time. I was dumbstruck—couldn't believe my eyes! Finally, two shots later, he fell into the bloodied water and this time stayed down.

Twelve shots! To his flanks, his shoulders, lungs, back, and neck!

What might have happened without that providential trench does not bear thinking about.

Koti Manga Camp, northern Cameroon, 2006

Broken Horn

Northern Cameroon

*The Lord Derby eland is the most fabulous of all
the African antelope—mysterious, unpredictable, and
tireless, and it possesses the keenest of senses.*
Michel Kaouche, professional hunter

In 2002 and 2003 we were told a herd of Lord Derby eland had been seen wandering in the hunting area of Koti Manga in northern Cameroon, which I often visited. The lead bull had only one horn, a distinction that had spared him the attention of trophy-seeking hunters and served as a kind of life insurance, allowing him to grow peacefully to a ripe old age and quite an exceptional size.

I had already shot several eland in this fabulous territory of some two hundred and fifty thousand acres between the Faro and Benue National Parks south of Garoua. I soon realized that I was expected to show an interest in this unusual head disdained by other hunters.

In 2004 this eland, which I nicknamed the Unicorn, had been spotted pretty much all over: in the south close to the banks of the Dogba, in the north on the slopes of Hossere Boumba, and in the east near Mayo Sala. He was reputed to be a huge animal, very dark in color, with a large dewlap that hung low to the ground. Unfortunately, despite many days of searching, we were unable to corner him.

We had no better luck the following year. I briefly caught sight of him only on the last day of the safari as he came charging out of a copse of Isoberlinia, prudently surrounded by his herd.

"It was Broken Horn, no doubt about it."

160

In 2006, no sooner had I arrived at camp than I was told that Broken Horn, as the others called him, had been sighted a number of times all over the area. Naturally, he had grown even bigger and, if the trackers were to be believed, now weighed over a ton! This time my reputation was at stake, and the whole team was ready and waiting for me, resolved to set out once more after Broken Horn. But he duped us yet again and remained invisible.

Africans often compare these legendary antelope to phantoms; never was a comparison more appropriate! Our animal had a particularly uncanny ability to vanish nimbly into thin air just as suddenly as he had appeared. So in January 2007, when I was jubilantly welcomed to the camp with the news that Broken Horn was still around, I did not show much enthusiasm. That would change.

At first light on day one, our best tracker, Gadal, a member of the Bororo tribe, pointed out the print of a "big foot" on the ground. The size made it stand out from all the others.

"It is him . . . Broken Horn!" he shouted in excitement.

Eland abounded in the area, and despite my confidence in this remarkable tracker, I was chastened by my previous defeats and rather skeptical.

The herd had a good start on us, and catching up required a long five-hour trek. About sixty animals had stopped in the shade of some trees. Most of them lay on the dry grass resting, except for a few older cows that stood alert, keeping watch.

Concealed in the vegetation of a small *mayo*, we had trouble identifying the animals, even through our binoculars. They were almost entirely hidden by the tall grass, only their long horns emerging from the sea of waving fronds. It was difficult to distinguish the horns from the branches and impossible to determine whether Broken Horn was among the group. Although we were downwind, we were going to have to sit and wait it out.

After an hour or two, as we lay patiently waiting on a mattress of leaves, a few animals began to stir. Gradually the herd came to life. The bush wasn't very thick here, and as they got up on their long legs it became easier to get a good look at them. With ceremonious deliberation, the magnificent antelope prepared to continue on their never-ending journey, changing the vast Koti Manga plateau, which just moments before had seemed totally deserted, into a spectacular stage that would have dwarfed anything but the huge eland.

161

Broken Horn, a.k.a. "the Unicorn" with my wife and South African professional hunter Danie Strydom.

Suddenly Gadal whispered, "Look, there he is, way over there!"

It was Broken Horn, no doubt about it. Despite the distance, he stood out from the others—regal with his long, charcoal-dark neck, impressive white-flecked dewlap, and a chestnut coat streaked with lighter stripes, which just seemed to add to his size.

When my shot rang out, the herd galloped off, leaving behind the staggering silhouette of their old leader, whose strength was rapidly failing. As I ran toward him, the team at my heels, our eyes met and I will never forget the look he gave me: Deep in those eyes I believe I saw anger and resignation.

I hastened to deliver the coup de grace. He collapsed, his single horn pointing toward the infinite African sky as if in an ultimate gesture of defiance. Now the *yamoussa* lay dead on a bed of ash left by the recent bush fires that frequently burn over the savanna.

I noticed that the old eland's muzzle was spattered with mud. Michel had once told me that this was the mark of a leader, a sign that he was the dominant male of the herd. Eland, he said, like buffalo and many other herbivores, prefer to drink at muddy watering holes where vegetation is sparse, rather than from the clear water of the rivers, whose banks are densely overgrown and offer good cover for large predators such as lion, leopard, and especially crocodile.

When a herd of eland—which might be sixty or more strong—arrives at a watering hole after a long day's journeying in the hot sun, the powerful, dominant males take their time drinking and then rubbing their faces in the mud for protection against the insects that constantly assail them. Then the cows and the young must hurry and drink quickly, hustled by the laggards and drawn onward by the lead bulls, which, their thirst slaked, are already on the move again, pushing toward the horizon.

Wasting no time, the Africans were getting ready to butcher the giant antelope. I sat a little to one side in the shade of an old acacia. I thought things over and couldn't help feeling that Broken Horn's death had deprived us of a dream. By killing the legend, we had broken the spell.

Koti Manga Camp, northern Cameroon, January 2007

The Buffalo of Lake Cabora Bassa

Mozambique

To Denis Verspieren, who was there . . .

*W*hat could possibly be going through the old Cape buffalo's head, I wondered, as he watched the large orangy-red sphere come up over the horizon, just as it did every day. That ball of fire was the color of blood, like the blood that had spurted from the mouth of the big baboon that the bull had seen a leopard kill the previous night.

The new day breaking in this desolate corner of Africa was a day like any other, a fragment of eternity. It was the end of the austral summer, and the implacable months-long drought was inexorably reducing the soil and vegetation to a field of ash where only the centuries-old giant baobab trees still stood fast. Reaching up to the sky, they stood proudly in a landscape otherwise stripped of all adornment.

The vegetation of the Zambezi Valley, on the other hand, remained lush. It formed a long and sinuous furrow, the water illuminated by the iridescent reflections of a multitude of different shades of green that the surrounding brown and ochre expanses threatened to engulf. Seen from above, it looked like a painting by Rothko, the uncontested master of American abstract expressionism.

The strange pale star that lights the bush so brightly at night, and seems to match the shape of the mighty lion's eye, had traveled many times across the starry heavens since that day long ago when the old bull was a calf wriggling from his mother's womb. Now the other bulls of the herd were waiting for an opportunity to chase him off to join the *dagga* boys, the old deposed males

The sun rises over the African bush.

that are excluded from the herds and who loiter around their edges covered in mud. What set this animal off from the other bulls was his crown, or the helmet formed by the joined protuberances at the base of his horns, which only the very old bulls possess. Whereas the coal-black hide of his young rivals was supple and shiny, his own graying hide was dull and rough and revealed a bony, emaciated frame. In Africa, almost more than anywhere else, time is a merciless master—for both man and beast.

The bull moved slowly among his herd, his head hanging low, as though weighted down. Like the other members of the group, he gleaned meager sustenance from dry leaves, straw, or bark from trees that had been felled by the elephant, themselves in search of fodder.

The herd stopped for a moment to drink at one of the rare watering holes that remained in this arid region. Some of the more powerful bulls took the opportunity to cover themselves with mud to keep off the tsetse flies that harassed them without respite. Like large antelope, the buffalo prefer the miry water of the watering holes to the clear water of the rivers, where the lion and crocodile lurk.

As he rounded a hamlet of miserable huts huddled together like large termite hills, the old bull detected the scent of the dark-skinned villagers, a combination of musk and cold ash. It was a familiar smell and did not alarm him. It was nothing like the sour, deadly stench that lingered in the wake of the light-skinned men who sometimes made noisy incursions into the bush and whom all the animals, from time immemorial, associated with imminent danger. As a calf he had followed his mother in the midst of the herd he was destined to lead one day, and learned the tough lesson of survival. The hated smell had almost always been associated with the death of one of the large bulls of the herd. Many moons before, his own father had been suddenly struck down just as the feared odor reached them, borne by the wind that stirred up the dust of the trail.

Once, a terrifying blast, louder than a thunderclap and more powerful than the lion's roar, had preceded the fierce sting of a strange insect that whistled like the fearsome mamba does when it is angry. Blood had spurted from his back. The wound had bled much more than when he'd injured himself driving away the presumptuous young bulls that lusted after his females.

166

Like all aged buffalo, the old cows that were responsible for the safety of the herd had poor eyesight and relied only on their keen sense of smell. They advanced, nostrils to the wind, ready to sound the alert at the slightest hint of danger.

Even now a group of the light-skinned hunters had discovered the buffalo's spoor and had been tracking them for a good while. From time to time one of them kicked the ground with the tip of his leather-shod foot to stir up the dust and see which way the wind was blowing. The trackers who accompanied them studied the innumerable hoofprints in the rust-colored earth, among which those of the big bull stood out because of their uncommon size.

The men progressed in silence at a cautious, steady pace; they knew they were nearing their prey and wanted to take it by complete surprise— "See before we're seen," said one of them, who seemed to be the leader of the group.

The fiery orb blazed above the bush, pale yellow now but blinding, unbearably bright. By the time it completed most of its journey across a sky whitened by

the heat haze rising from the warm river, the herd had begun to zigzag across the plain in search of shade to await the return of the cooler temperatures of evening. The youngest animals dropped down in the dry grass; the others ruminated peacefully, standing as still as statues in the dappled shade of the foliage. They blended in with the vegetation but betrayed their presence by the swishing of their tails to drive away the flies.

But one cow, the wariest one, slightly apart from the others, appeared uneasy. She was on the alert, shaking her head nervously from side to side, peering back intently at the path they had taken. She was particularly puzzled by the behavior of the honeyguide, a curious bird known to Africans as "the indicator." Several times she thought she had heard the shrill cry of this strange bird the size of a large sparrow, whose *cheek-kerr, cheek-kerr* sounds like the squeaky pulley of a village well, with none of the melodious trill of Mozambique's yellow-eyed canary.

In the course of the honeyguide's evolution, nature has smiled upon the mischievous little bird, allowing it to align its own way of life with that of the human honey-seekers who, from time immemorial, have relentlessly combed the woods of the savanna in search of wild beehives. For indeed, while their more sophisticated cousins in other parts of the world have the good fortune to reside in handsome little "cottages," African bees stash their honey deep inside hollows in the highest trees, making it very difficult for humans to find it.

Now, the honeyguide, on the other hand, knows exactly where to find the simple hives, which are staunchly defended by their owners. And thus for thousands of years, perhaps since as far back as the Pliocene period, honey-seekers and indicator birds have been helping each other out. The cunning little bird gradually became accustomed to guiding early man toward the hideaways where the bees store their precious nectar, receiving a small part of the booty in return for its valuable collaboration.

Perched at the top of a tree on the outskirts of a village, the bird observes the villagers as they enter the forest and tries to catch their attention with its screechy *cheek-kerr, cheek-kerr*. This call has the collateral effect of signaling the presence of dangerous humans to all the other animals around, which have learned over time to associate the bird's hysterical shrieking with imminent danger.

168

A superb trophy—an old Cape buffalo with a well-developed helmet—lies where he was shot at the edge of Lake Cabora Bassa in October 2007.

The old cow buffalo knew instinctively that the call of the honeyguide meant trouble. As soon as she caught sight of it flying from tree to tree, squawking and making a great display of flapping wings, she bellowed in fright and set off at a great gallop with her tail across her back and the rest of the herd in tow, in a crash of broken branches and clashing stones.

But it was too late: An explosion that seemed to emerge from deep within the earth smothered all other sounds. This time, the repeated warnings of his comrade, the honeyguide, had not managed to save the old bull. He never even felt the sting of the huge, copper-winged bee as it pierced his chest. He fell dead on the spot, his noble helmet stained with the blood that spurted from his chest.

Deep in the bush the young bulls were already fighting among themselves for the females that were theirs for the taking now that the old king was dead. Down where the earth and the sky meet, the sun had reclaimed its crimson colors of early dawn and was dropping fast into the deep waters of Lake Cabora Bassa.

Lake Cabora Bassa, Mozambique, 2007

Surprises in Koti Manga

Northern Cameroon

In the African bush, the unusual, the extraordinary,
may surprise you at any moment.

Michel Kaouche, professional hunter

A few days before leaving for northern Cameroon at the beginning of January 2008, I called Michel. "Make sure you don't get your eland on the very first day of the safari," he said laughingly.

Michel had always believed that this regal antelope offered the very best big-game hunting on the savanna and felt that killing one early on in the hunt would take away much of the interest of the rest of the safari. In this belief he was quite right. He preferred to savor the thrill, make it last, observe the herds, search out the best trophies—"do the inventory" as he used to say. I would point out that doing it his way risked losing our "bird in the hand." But he would ignore my comments, or make fun of my protestations. He had seen many eland and was in no hurry.

"To get a really great trophy," he would say, "you have to try to see all of them and not go for the first one like a novice."

By 2008 the times were long gone when Michel and I scoured the vast semidesert plains of Central Africa and northern Cameroon together in search of the magnificent antelope, and I readily admit that without my old friend it felt as though the hunt was lacking something. It was not the same. Yet such is life: The older we get, the more good friends we leave along the wayside. Some are gone forever; others head off on a different path. We usually end up alone, finishing as we started out.

Bushpig shot on the banks of the Bamingui River in northern Central African Republic. Notice its handsome, silky, orangy coat shot through with silver-tipped charcoal hairs. The two huge warts on either side of the snout indicate that this is an old male.

Mindful of Michel's recommendations, I promised myself not to go shooting my eland on the very first day. And yet, on the very first day, shortly after we had zeroed our guns, a large herd of the majestic antelope passed a couple of hundred yards away from our camp, as if issuing us a challenge.

Hiding as best we could behind a clump of scraggly bushes, we observed the giant eland. There may have been sixty of them, perhaps even more! But they were difficult to count, scattered as they were over a wide area among the bushes and tall, dry grasses. As usual, we could not see the large bulls; they generally stick to the center of the herd, where they feel safe from danger.

Once evening came, the antelope appeared more confident. I had many times before observed how, as dusk falls, the big-game animals drop their guard a little. Perhaps they imagine that the treachery of man, their worst enemy, recedes with the waning light of day. In any case, it had almost always been at this moment of the day that I was able to witness their private moments, their courting, the playful fighting of the "young chiefs." It was also the time of day when the calves, nudging hard at their mother's bellies, suckled the last drops of milk to be had.

Less than a stone's throw from where we were hidden, a young bull was courting a cow. Heedless, the two lovers had moved away from the herd and were heading straight toward us. I watched peaceably from where I sat on the ground, having made up my mind that I would do nothing to disturb their tryst. The other members of my party—my wife, Maria Dolores; Guillaume, a young apprentice guide; Zimbabwean professional hunter and friend Scott Guthrie; and the three trackers—sat close-by, somewhat surprised and frustrated by my unexpected passivity.

The cow in heat was now very close. Completely absorbed in her courtship, she was not aware of us. I knew, though, that it would be only a few more yards before she caught wind of us. Luckily, she stopped just before crossing the invisible line beyond which she would certainly have picked up our scent and immediately fled, along with the rest of the herd.

It was becoming clear that she was on the point of succumbing to the advances of her handsome young swain when from the bushes a second bull . . . and then a third and a fourth . . . came to join the couple. I stayed stock-still, my rifle resting against a small acacia. I could feel my fellow hunters' eyes riveted on me, but, although I could well imagine their impatience, it did not in the least

"In measuring a bushpig for trophy purposes, the length and circumference of the tusks are used. The first measurements of my pigs were taken in situ by a professional hunter who was an official measurer for Safari Club International. The results? The first animal rated a gold medal and a place in the world's top twenty, and the second received a silver medal. Who could ask for more!"

lessen my resolve. It was extraordinary to see these four males competing for the favors of the object of their desires. I had never seen anything like it before, and it was priceless.

As I watched, rapt, there suddenly appeared from out of nowhere one of the finest specimens of Lord Derby eland I had ever seen in my life. Clearly this was the dominant male, intent on claiming his rights as master of the harem and driving away the other suitors. He was a majestic beast, with thick, black, spiraling horns so long that they rubbed against his withers when he raised his head in a gesture of intimidation to his younger rivals. It was just too much! The fates were conspiring, tempting and goading me.

Gadal, the first tracker, grabbed my gun and held it out to me. Guillaume looked across at me, and Maria Dolores sent me a ravishing smile, nailing the fate of the eland. He fell with a bullet to the base of the neck, a victim of his love for the beautiful damsel.

The sun was setting, illuminating the vast Koti Manga plateau for a few moments longer with its last slanting rays. Gradually the dark evening shadow of the surrounding hills spread across the area like a shroud.

We had killed the eland on the first day of the hunt, and now we needed to find a new goal for our safari. Buffalo, roan, and hartebeest were plentiful, but I was no longer interested. What I wanted was something more unusual, something rare. Talking it over with the trackers, I learned that a sounder of bushpigs had been observed on several occasions in one of the more remote sectors of the hunting area.

Even though there are many more of them than one might think, bushpigs are shy animals and it is no easy thing to get one in your sights. The few times in the past when I had actually managed to shoot one, it had been more of a fluke than anything else.

Bushpigs are nocturnal and live in the thick *bako*s, leaving only under cover of darkness and returning at the first light of dawn. Unlike their cousins, the ugly warthog and the monstrous giant forest hog, these medium-size swine (the males rarely weigh more than two hundred and twenty pounds) have a thick, silky coat that is orangy in color with mahogany highlights and agreeably shot through with rather smart, silver-tipped charcoal hairs.

At first light on the following day, my suggestion that we try to find some of these vaunted pigs by tracking them as one does buffalo and giant antelope met with the unbridled enthusiasm of the whole team. It would be no easy undertaking, for the bushpigs had taken up residence in a huge forest some two to three square miles in area, where they had left a confusion of new and old tracks. As we progressed through the dense underbrush, I began to think that we stood more chance of finding a needle in a haystack than of coming face to face with a bushpig.

I cast a sidelong glance at Gadal, our best tracker. Confident, he made his way unerringly through the maze of tunnels the wild pigs had bored through the undergrowth with all their comings and goings. When he found it impossible to read the tracks on the ground, he would sniff the wind like one of the big predators and follow his nose.

The more time passed, the more doubtful I was of any chance of success. I was about to sound the retreat when, just as we least expected it, we caught sight of a large boar concealed in the thick, dark vegetation. He appeared to be observing us curiously, probably intrigued by the intrusion of strange two-legged beasts into his inhospitable home that he thought impregnable.

A quick shot was followed by lots of blood and a chase that lasted all of ten or fifteen seconds. We saw the fugitive head off into the foliage, and a second, very lucky shot got the better of the animal. It was an old boar with long tusks and huge warts on either side of his snout.

Delighted with the kill, the Africans proudly announced that no bushpig had been shot in the area in many a long year, a fact that evidently added to their satisfaction.

Meanwhile, I was examining the dead animal and was nonplussed to find a single bullet wound instead of the two I had expected. And for good reason: The bushpig lay dead just a few yards from a second bushpig that had been hit by my second shot, the unintended victim of a most unusual "miss." We had shot the two largest old hogs, a few seconds apart. Our African helpers were overjoyed, and threw themselves into a wild celebration of singing and dancing.

In measuring a bushpig for trophy purposes, the length and circumference of the tusks are used. The first measurements of my pigs were taken *in situ* by a professional hunter who was an official measurer for Safari Club International. The results? The first animal was worthy of a gold medal and a place in the world's top twenty; the second rated a silver medal. Who could ask for more!

Koti Manga Camp, northern Cameroon, January 2008

Hunting with the Baka Pygmies in the Rain Forest

Kounabembe Camp,
Yokadouma Region, Southern Cameroon

If your God is dead, take mine. He's truly alive!
African Proverb

After being content for a while to utter relentless rumblings, the heavens opened and unleashed a long-pent-up flood of warm water upon us. A soft, warm wind blew across the treetops of the tropical forest. The incredible tangle of giant trunks, intertwined vines, and creepers formed a wall of vegetation so dense that we could see only occasional flickerings of daylight through the thick, olive-green canopy that hung fifty yards above our heads.

All this lent an almost surreal ambience to the strange world into which we had penetrated with some trepidation. The Pygmies led the way. They seemed completely oblivious of the torrential rain that was soaking us to the bone.

These diminutive people never cease to amaze me. Barely four and a half feet tall, they contemplate their world with the confidence born of the vast collective knowledge they have acquired since time immemorial, viewing with equanimity an environment so hostile it would have defeated any other human beings. They seem indefatigable and are possessed of a wonderful, unshakable ability to enjoy life to the fullest.

The rain coursed over their near-naked Lilliputian but well-proportioned bodies. Occasionally they looked back as though to make sure we had not been abducted by some malevolent spirit, and sent us broad, encouraging smiles, displaying the most splendid teeth I had seen in all of Africa.

History and millennia had not changed their mores. Nature supplied them with shelter and food, clothing, weapons, tools, and a precious pharmacopoeia. It protected them from the outside world, and they lived like Adam and Eve before they were banished from their earthly paradise. I am not certain they were even conscious of ever having been colonized, first by the Germans, then the French!

Observing them, I could not help thinking that we might learn a great deal from their way of life. But I also realized that I would have a hard time converting my "civilized" fellows (who were quite capable of getting all riled up if served Pepsi when they had ordered Coke). We moderns are hardly predisposed to look back to prehistoric times to rediscover how to enjoy life, an ability we have killed with all the rules imposed by our society, its economic demands, and so many other obligations.

What's more, the Pygmies do not pollute the natural world, and they take only what they need. For these people, the forest is the Mother, giver of life.

From time to time a shaft of lightning would streak through a gap in the foliage and illuminate the jungle floor, heightening the dreamlike quality of this fairy-tale setting. Our companions did not fear the anger of the skies. They put it down to the changing moods of the only god they recognized: Kumba, the almighty creator of their universe. To my great surprise, even as the storm was at its height, setting ablaze the uppermost reaches of the trees, the Pygmies broke into a traditional refrain, as if all were for the best in the best of all possible worlds.

Armed with their miniature crossbows and short lances that they proudly brandished as though they were machine guns, Tonga, the head tracker, and his comrades moved through this ocean of greenery with three or four mutts close on their heels. The animals looked more like jackals than hunting dogs, given their mangy hides, torn ears, beady eyes, and turned-up tails—except for one that had a black coat and a docked tail. Deido, that one's owner, explained to me that his grandfather had been killed by an *ebobo* while out gathering wild mangoes in the forest. The poor man's dog had tried courageously to defend its master, but the gorilla had grabbed it by the tail and dashed it against a mango tree, splitting open its skull. Ever since then, the Bagando tribe to which Deido belonged had cut off the tails of their hunting dogs to

Baka hunter on the lookout for monkeys, crossbow at the ready.

spare them a similar fate. The pack was a sorry sight. Moreover, the curs, like their masters, seemed more interested in the gibbering monkeys that were teasing us from up in their perches than in the elusive bongo we sought—of which we had so far seen nary a one.

The fact is that our safari companions loved monkey meat, as do all Africans, and considered it to be tastier, more nourishing, and better-textured than any other. We had a hard time getting them to focus on their mission, which was to lead us to the bongo, the mysterious antelope that is so difficult to flush out in this almost impenetrable jungle.

A few days before flying out to southern Cameroon I had called Michel, as I usually did, to tell him about my plans.

"It wasn't so long ago that I was there, in Yokadouma," he commented offhandedly, trying to sound indifferent. Then, after a short silence, he went on, "Yes, I led elephant safaris there about—ah, hum—forty-five years ago."

"Just yesterday, huh?" I shot back at him in the same tone, before he added in a neutral voice, though I did detect a trace of his hallmark irony, "By the way, don't forget that female bongo have horns too."

What was that supposed to mean? Was he saying that without him I might mistakenly shoot a female, or had he himself had just such a misadventure forty-five years before?

"In any case, there's no danger of you falling for a Pygmy woman. They're not your type, or mine either for that matter!"

And that was all I could get out of him. The subject was closed and the remainder of our conversation was on ordinary matters, nothing to do with big-game hunting, or Africa, or even women—black or white. But I was aware that the slender thread that connected my friend to Africa had not yet been entirely severed and that, even if he gave nothing away, his innermost thoughts turned, more often than he would like to admit, to the infinite plains of Africa.

It took us more than six hours to make our way through the muddy swamps, where we had to use our machetes to cut a path in the dense vegetation. We finally reached a small Pygmy village that had been abandoned many moons before.

As night was falling, our men set to fixing up as best they could the little huts, shaped like upside-down bells and covered with large dried leaves set in a pattern reminiscent of the shell of a sea turtle. A meager fire was lit—I don't know how, so humid was the air. We shared a frugal meal and burrowed into our damp sleeping bags.

We had all been asleep for several hours when an incredibly violent storm broke out, unleashing a volley of explosions and bursts of lightning that lit up the small clearing in which we had taken refuge. The gigantic trees creaked under the heavy winds lashing their tops, and torrents of water came crashing down on our fragile shelters. In all my life I had never experienced such a storm!

When day broke, the anger of Kumba, god of the forest, abated and spangles of sun pierced the canopy, falling on us like the golden rain on Danae. Our men emerged from the huts one after another, their faces haggard with fear. Only the five Pygmies, who took such meteorological phenomena in their stride, bore their usual serene, relaxed demeanor. I was enchanted by these little men that nothing seemed to faze.

One of them leaped out of the foliage surrounding us and announced that he had found fresh spoor of a herd of bongo just a few minutes' walk from our makeshift camp. The news bucked us up and we set off forthwith.

After two hours of laborious tracking in that hostile environment, Tonga came to a halt and whispered, "There they are!"

How the devil could he know that? Our vision was limited to a few yards at most. He saw me looking skeptical and touched his nose with the index finger of his left hand. His right hand tightly clutched his little crossbow, on which sat a poison-tipped arrow[1]. Then I realized that Tonga had scented rather than seen the bongo. The dogs too had smelled the mysterious antelope. Sniffing the wind, their flanks quivering, they strained against the slender ropes of vine that held them at bay. At a sign from their chief, the men loosed the dogs, which immediately took off into the thick brush. There followed a concert of barking, a mad chase through a tangled maze of brambles, bushes, and branches, and suddenly the mythical creature was before us, just a few steps away. It seemed completely indifferent to our presence, busy as it was with the hounds leaping at its throat.

---

[1]Tonga later gave me this ingenious weapon. It has pride of place among the memorabilia displayed in the African room of my country home in the Limousin, in central France.

Baka Pygmies have captured a small nguendi *antelope (Peters duiker). One of them carries at*
they have cut down. With their small axes, like the one carried on the shoulder of the next-to-la

his waist two bags made of leaves and filled with honey collected from a wild beehive in a tree
man, they can chop down a 100-foot-tall tree in a few hours.

Its dark, chestnut-colored coat with sharply drawn white stripes was shiny, the effect heightened by the brilliant varnish of dew that coated us all. Using its massive, spiraling horns, it was trying bravely to fend off the hounds attacking it from all sides.

It was a female—an elegant female sacrificing herself so that the rest of the herd could escape the ferocious pack that was about to rip her to shreds. My eyes were riveted to the sight—she was so beautiful and so brave.

We had a difficult time persuading the Pygmy hunters to call off their canines and spare the poor animal that was about to be slaughtered without any consideration given to its sex. When they finally did call back their dogs, the female bongo moved off calmly, looking like a lady who had been hustled by a bunch of drunken louts and who, after patting her hair back into place, continued on her way stately and dignified.

At that moment I thought back with a smile to Michel and his tongue-in-cheek warning: "Female bongo have horns too."

Had he cast one of those old African spells on me? Was I perhaps not allowed to succeed without him? I couldn't help being amused. No self-respecting hunter kills females.

A female bongo sacrificing herself for the herd.

The following days were exhausting. The Pygmies led us on arduous treks through the primary forest. At every stop we were assailed by swarms of bees, and if we let down our guard for but a moment, squadrons of magnan ants would crawl inside our clothes and sink their powerful mandibles into our flesh. And as if that were not enough, we were constantly drenched.

From time to time the Pygmies would leave us for a few hours and come back laden with honey, which they collected by simply hacking down huge trees without any scruples whatsoever, using their primitive axes. One day they returned with a black-striped duiker they had probably captured in one of their traps or perhaps with the help of their intrepid hunting dogs. Around a fire that produced more smoke than flame—which at least had the advantage of warding off insects—they skinned the animal and we devoured it together hungrily, starved as we were for fresh meat.

Sitting among the buttress roots of a one-hundred-and-thirty-foot Sipo tree, I watched and listened as they sang. My friend Deido translated for me:

Doumo invited pretty Yambi
To gather honey in the forest with him.
With a vine he tied her up, and then he stripped her bare.
Doumo cut the vine and Yambi began to run.
But he caught her, and beneath the Bubinga tree
He mounted her like Souha the leopard.

All around us the air twinkled with fireflies. Had the god Kumba sent them to make up for depriving us of stars for so long? In any case, that is what is told in one of the many legends of the rich Baka mythology.

The silence of the night was rent by a loud rumbling, an eerie groan that suddenly became the loud crash of falling timber. One of the giants had come down, defeated by time, termites, and tropical storms. Such were the harrowing death throes of the Bubinga, Sipo, mahogany, umbrella, and Sapelli trees.

Was the forest sending me a message? This day, 27 June 2008, was my sixty-fifth birthday. How long it had been since I began wandering the wadis of the Hoggar with the fierce Tuareg warriors! What was I doing here, so far from my loved ones, lying on the ground on a bed of leaves, my body aching, my arms

This beautiful bongo trophy was taken in the rain forest of southeastern Cameroon, June 2009.

187

and legs bruised, scratched, and covered in insect bites? What was this incredible hold Africa had on me?

Night was taking leave of us. Bit by bit the song of the calao bird replaced the chirping of the cicadas. Another day was breaking over the equatorial forest, and I was ready to set off yet again on the trail of the great solitary bongo.

Yokadouma region, southern Cameroon, June 2008

Epilogue

I would come back to where it pleased me to live;
to really live. Not just let my life pass.

Ernest Hemingway
Green Hills of Africa

And so, Dear Reader, we have come to the end of our forty-year-long odyssey across the vast African continent.

In the north—in the Hoggar Mountains, heart of the Sahara—we were among the last to hunt the small dorcas gazelle that are now almost extinct. We traveled with the nomadic Tuareg, lords of the desert, who are now becoming more and more sedentary.

Since 1966, when we had the honor of representing France at the fiftieth anniversary of the death of Father de Foucauld, the lovely little town of Tamanrasset, with its buildings of red clay smothered in bright bougainvillea, has been invaded by a constant influx of immigrants from subtropical Africa. These new inhabitants have created abominable shantytowns, heedlessly disfiguring the once-attractive town. The caravan trails that converged here from all over the continent have now become roads potholed by the constant flow of heavy vehicles that have replaced the camel caravans of the past. The former picturesque camel market is now a common parking lot, littered with the filth left by countless trucks.

Farther south, we made several trips to the Central African Republic, once among the most beautiful hunting areas in the whole of central Africa. In a period of less than two decades we have seen it become a veritable desert, at least as regards hunting, especially its northeastern regions. It has been repeatedly battered by Sudanese militia, who, equipped with military weapons, horses, and camels, have mercilessly massacred the buffalo, elephant, and large antelope.

Over to the west, Cameroon has learned to protect its wildlife—one of the most varied collections on the whole continent. In northern Cameroon we tracked Lord Derby eland in the woodland savanna of Adamaoua, and in the primary forest of the country's far south the Pygmies welcomed us and taught us how to hunt bongo, sitatunga, and duiker according to their ancestral traditions. Over the years, we have witnessed the preservation of Cameroon's fabulous fauna, and in some cases even seen it increase.

Looking eastward, Tanzania, bathed by the Indian Ocean, offered us breathtaking views of the Rift Valley, called the cradle of mankind, and its sumptuous national parks: Serengeti, Lake Manyara, Ngorongoro Crater, and Kilimanjaro with its everlasting snows, to mention but the most well known. We took record trophies—lesser kudu, gerenuk, Grant and Thomson gazelle, fringe-eared oryx. . . .

Our memories of the Great Lakes region are filled with sadness when we think back to our trip to Rwanda, land of the Tutsis, the "Masters of Africa." We were there not so very long before that little paradise was plunged into the horror of the most barbaric genocide.

Our journeys also took us to Zimbabwe in southern Africa, to the foot of the matchless Victoria Falls, discovered by Livingstone in the mid-nineteenth century. Despite the madness of President Mugabe's catastrophic leadership, Zimbabwe has remained a fabulous animal Eden where elephant, buffalo, big cats, and other species abound.

Let us not forget Mozambique, one of the world's poorest states. It is slowly recovering from the damage of a twenty-year-long civil war as senseless as it was destructive. Today Mozambique is working hard, and with a certain measure of success, to build itself back up into the magnificent hunting territory it was in the days before it threw off the yoke of Portuguese colonization.

It may be surprising to some that I have not mentioned South Africa at all. I admit that our visit there was rather short, largely because the hunting seemed to be a bit too "organized" for our taste. It is a superb destination that we will save for a time, inexorably drawing closer, when age no longer allows us to be as adventurous as we once were.

My wife, Maria Dolores, with her SCI silver medal Thomson gazelle, taken in the Longido area, Masailand, 2006.

This short retrospective would be incomplete without a mention of Botswana. Due to an unfortunate incident, we didn't make it to the Okavango Delta. The Okavango River loses itself in the sands of the Kalahari Desert, creating lush vegetation that forms one of the most beautiful landscapes in the whole of creation and is home to every animal existing in this part of Africa.

Missing Botswana is my only regret! But perhaps one day . . . God willing, as the Africans are wont to say.

One thing is certain: Africa today is no longer the Africa I once knew. Slowly it is evolving, modernizing. Every day paved roads creep farther into the bush, and almost everywhere the traditional tribal chiefs have been replaced by corrupt, pettifogging civil servants.

My wife and I with a white-bearded wildebeest, Masailand, Tanzania, 2006.

In just a few decades the continent's population has more than doubled. Overgrazing, deforestation, and the depletion of water resources are threatening irreversible desertification in vast territories that, not so long ago, were famed for their fertility. The Africans live crowded along metaled roads in dreary, characterless communities strewn with garbage amid general indifference.

With a few exceptions (including northern Cameroon, the southern part of Burkina Faso, and some mountainous areas of Ethiopia), most of the vast stretches that lie north of the fifth parallel—more than half the continent's surface—are home to only a scant residual fauna that struggle for survival. And south of the fifth parallel: Are the management and protection of big game a primary concern of all the countries there? What is happening to the fauna of the Democratic Republic of Congo or of Angola, to mention but two of the biggest of those states?

The rare big game that still survives outside the few remaining sanctuaries is relentlessly hunted by unscrupulous poachers—and quite often by professional hunters with dubious ethics. In some African countries hunters shoot lion, buffalo, and kudu without even leaving their vehicles, in reserves enclosed by high fences where the noble creatures are corralled like common cattle.

Like the rest of the world, sub-Saharan Africa is changing, and not for the better. Rwanda, the Democratic Republic of the Congo, Nigeria, Zimbabwe, Sudan, Ethiopia, Liberia, Sierra Leone, Chad, Uganda, the Central African Republic, Ivory Coast . . . the list of countries where civil war and tyrannical obscurantism hold sway gets ever longer.

Only a handful of countries have finally realized that the preservation and management of their wildlife represent an enormous asset. As part of this concept, carefully managed big-game hunting has an important role to play. One does not need to be clairvoyant to predict that the value of this priceless treasure will but increase with time, and that its preservation is in the best interests of all humankind.

When I travel in Europe I often stop off to visit Michel, who lives alone in his country house near Bar-le-Duc in northeastern France. We only rarely speak of our times together in this lost paradise, unconsciously afraid, perhaps, of marring the memories that we carry in our hearts. In the face of history, we are but so much dust blown by the wind along the paths of adventure.

Zoumbala outside his hut on the banks of the Bamingui River.

And many winds have blown over the plateaus of Kaga Nze and Koti Manga, over the savanna of the Selous and the Rift Valley since the day I jotted down the first lines of this African chronicle. Each storm, each mad whirlwind, has swept away a little more of the rich soil in which the traditions and legends of Africa are rooted. As the world grows smaller, there is less and less space for the big herds of wild animals and for big, exhilarating ideals.

I'm afraid I have not been blessed with even a grain of the talent Providence so generously bestowed on Ernest Hemingway, Joseph Conrad, and Romain Gary, but from time to time—more and more often, if truth be told—I lose myself in *Breath of Africa*. Its pages take me back to Zoumbala, Yando, Haman, Issa, and my other African comrades. I wonder what has become of them. Some, I fear, will have gone to join their ancestors in far-off places, where they are sure to have met up with Karen Blixen, Frederick Courteney Selous, and many of our other departed friends.

But Africa, by the grace of God, is eternal, enduring, even if she sometimes appears to be headed down the road to ruin. The elephant, the buffalo, and the giant eland will survive for many years to come. Long after we are gone, the majestic herds will continue to roam the vast expanses of the Central Plateau where, I can only hope, a big old lion will always prowl, his deep and mighty roar calling the first spark of dawn to return each day to revive the souls of the ghosts of the past.

Zoumbala never returned to call the lion on the slopes of Mount Doukoua. From time to time I imagine him as older, lost in his thoughts, squatting on a mat outside a poor hut on the banks of the Bamingui River, far away on the high Central African plateau.

At times when I give my nostalgia free rein, it does seem to me that my heart beats a little faster. Before time erases everything, it pleases me to believe that Zoumbala still thinks of us.

Lausanne, Switzerland, July 2008

Glossary

Glossary

A

Akli	Black servant.
Alenkad	Gazelle, in Tamahaq.
Amenokal	Tuareg overlord.

B

Bako	Thick forest.
Bamileke	Tribe of the western high plateaus of Cameroon.
Banda	Tribe of Central African Republic, of Sudanese origin.
Baroga	Lion, in Fulfulde, language of the Fulbe.
Bassa	Tribe of southern Cameroon.
Biltong	Strips of dried meat.
Bodiman	Tribe related to the Bassa, living on the banks of the Wouri River.
Bororo	Tribe of northern Cameroon.
Bosobo	Eland, in Sango.
Boukarou	Thatched mud hut.

C

Choa	Tribe of Chad and northern Cameroon.
Chui	Panther, or leopard, in Swahili.

D

Dagga	Mud in Shona, a Bantu language. Old buffalo bulls are called *dagga* boys.
Duru	Tribe of northern Cameroon.

Ɛ

Ebobo	Gorilla.

F

Fulbe	Ethnic group of northern Cameroon and other countries around the tenth parallel.
Fulfulde	Language of the Fulbe.

G

Gandura	Ample tunic worn in North Africa.
Gri-gri	Charm, fetish, or amulet.
Guelta	A watering hole that never dries up.

H

Harmattan	A dry and dust-laden West African wind.
Haratin	"Black Berbers" of North Africa, sedentary farmers of lower caste, often of mixed blood.
Hatari	Danger in Swahili.
Hossere	Mountain, in Fulfulde, language of the Fulbe.

Ɔ

Imrad	High-ranking Targui.

K

Koba	Antelope *(Hippotragus equinus)*.
Kola	Nut containing caffeine, used as a stimulant.
Korongo	Small, wooded ravine.

M

Matabele	Tribe of western Zimbabwe.
Mayo	Watercourse.
Mbogo	Buffalo, in Fulfulde.
Mehari	Camel.

N

Nyama	Meat, in Sango.

R

Razzia	Raid.
Reg	A desert plateau swept by violent winds that have blown away the sand, leaving vast plains of gravel and stones.

S

Sango	National language of Central African Republic, and lingua franca of Central Africa.
Sara	Tribe of Chad (Moussa belonged to this tribe).
Simoom	A hot, dry, and dust-laden wind that blows in the Sahara, Palestine, Jordan, Syria, and the deserts of the Arabian Peninsula.

T

Tamahaq	Original Berber language of the Tuareg.
Targui	Berber of North Africa (plural: Tuareg).

Tarik	(or Rhala) Tuareg dromedary saddle.
Tembo	Elephant in Swahili.
Tifinagh	Character of the Tamahaq alphabet.
Tuareg	Berber people of North Africa.

W

Wadi	Bed or valley of a stream, often dry except in the rainy season.

Y

Yamoussa	Eland, in Fulfulde.